Preface:

MW01250731

Musings on everyday life.

It is my intent to share thoughts that occur to me that are in ... y
everyday interactions into something we often cannot see and creating an
awakening to that around us all.

I have the hope that just one thought meets you where you are that particular day
and helps you reach for more in life, see more in what you bring to your life and
to find more peace right where you are.

I was inspired greatly by my wife Anna Maria, Ray Justice, Mark Nepo, Eckhart
Tolle, and those children that created MZEE; Awak, Achanti and Amora and our
lifelong friends from 3 Timbers - Connie, Craig, Laurie, Earl, Nancy, Paul, Amy,
Geoff, Anne and Ted, who challenge me deeply and give me pause to consider
this wonderful world and our role in it.

Author's story:

Jerry DeLuccio lives in Rochester, NY. He and his wife Anna Maria have been
blessed with a family that includes loved ones from South Sudan. In trips to
Africa and visits with tribal units, we learned of the supreme value of the MZEE,
the village elder.

The MZEE provides experience and wisdom to the young people of the tribe and
this wisdom is imparted and respected through stories.

Cover art:

The "Sun Arising" copyright 2013: Awak Thongjang

Chapter 1: January
JANUARY 1

Feeling your senses?

On every New Year, we face some intense feelings about what the future holds. How do we best explore them so that we can identify the truth versus the non-truth in our thinking and expand our possibilities?

Feeling our senses is a way to get around our everyday way of thinking and connecting and opening ourselves to see and feel more. It is mind opening to intentionally use a sense to do what it doesn't typically do? Like touch a flower with your eyes? Taste a wine with your nose?

We can do so much more than we know. It is this opening of your senses to the unusual that opens you to growing and feeling more, seeing more, sensing more and to better discern our truth. A perfect New Years message for us to hear.

The spirit lives in a quiet place behind the noise of our everyday routines. We are special beings, capable of sensing and knowing more, much more, and then taking our resolutions to new and exciting places.

Chapter 1: January
JANUARY 2

What is your role?

We rush through life assuming a role we assign ourselves or others assign for us...daddy, mommy, boss, bus driver, friend, lover, bully, loser. We find our worth or lack of worth in those roles we try and live into.

Often we act exclusively around our 'roles', not leaving time to sit with ourselves. We rush, we hit target dates, we go from meeting to meeting, from task to task and time is our enemy.

As we run around doing what we believe is absolutely critical, moments pass waiting to be discovered. I believe moments are where the divine calls us.

They are soft callings, like your child's facial expression, needing to sit with a lonely friend, listening to the story of a stranger put right into your path, watching a hummingbird feed. They deserve attention because they feed us differently.

Playing our roles inevitably causes us to miss these moments because we see them as unimportant if we see them at all. In effect, we are filling time playing our role, yet so very often we are not filled!

If we could strip the grip our roles have on our time, and look to experience the moments that come every day, we will find that we transcend time rather than finding time an enemy.

It is then we will desire to stay awhile and our roles become secondary, if only for that moment, but in that moment we touch something inside us that helps feed everything else we do.

Chapter 1: January
JANUARY 3

Are you done? Or becoming?

We all want to be done, complete, whole! We humans create a tension here in that we are achievement oriented and we seek a direct path to a final result most of the time.

We are beings too. As a "being", the path toward being done has to first go through becoming. That path is no longer a direct one because becoming is a counter intuitive process with no achievement goal or end result.

In becoming, we need to unlearn not learn! We need to break life's lessons apart so that we are free to find our true inner self behind the self we created and we know.

Becoming is a journey that transcends space and time and puts us face to face with unknowing and mystery. That is the tension.

So, as "beings" we likely will never be done but the journey toward becoming is the achievement we should seek.

Chapter 1: January
JANUARY 4

Is there a 'hardness' in us?

Reading the news makes it clear that we have room to be more compassionate as a people of this earth. How do we open ourselves to be more compassionate?

Can you picture your heart as the producer of compassion. Now picture it working like a soft sponge opening and closing with each beat? With each moment it opens and absorbs all that is around it, almost like becoming one with what it absorbs, then with a squeeze, it sends what it has absorbed out. In our bodies, that process is completed with the absorption or life giving blood and nutrients, in our lives that can be the giving and receiving of compassion.

Picture now a hardened sponge that can't absorb as well and can't be squeezed as much. The power to provide life giving nutrients diminishes. We are less alive and less capable of being compassionate.

So to overcome the hardness that we see or that we fear, we need to stay soft, be flexible, be easily squeezed and formed by the things around us, and open to accept all as worthy of distributing back into the universe.

Chapter 1: January
JANUARY 5

Are we an expression of God? OR are we just here?

We do not exist apart from all things. All things are a part of the miracle that we share as one.

When I have the pleasure to be out watching the night sky, the majesty of the stars, the moon, the quiet existence of all things creates a feeling of awe where I feel part of the miracle I am watching. I am not just here alone, I feel here in the midst of a miracle.

When we see ourselves like that, we become more ONE and more worthy. Just as a wave cannot separate from the ocean, or a note cannot be split away from the music, so we cannot be taken from our part to play in this world. We do not exist outside of everything else.

So we are not just here, we have unique value as one of God's unique instruments of expression. That makes us more special than we sometimes feel.

Chapter 1: January
JANUARY 6

Belonging

Is there a better feeling than knowing you belong? In all our differences as people of the world, we are knitted together into one tapestry. Like a flute with infinite holes, or a wave in the mighty ocean, or a particle of sand on the ocean floor - we are one where we belong to the whole. That might be a sobering thought to you, but by definition, the whole is not the whole without us, so the thought of not belonging is merely a thought that should not exist!

Chapter 1: January
JANUARY 7

The yin and the yang!

The popular Buddhist theory of energy conveys what exactly to us? I bring a varied and larger perspective to that yin/yang within us. I believe they represent more than energy of a single spirit, and that in a similar fashion reflect the energy of the ONENESS of all peoples.

In the greatest unity of ONE spirit, we balance each other in the whole and as a microcosm we balance ourselves as well in doing our part.

If the yin and the yang are two sides of our true oneness - when we are balanced we are more one with the world and we see our overall oneness more clearly.

In world crises, we see this in action. It amazes us that so many people help and offer heroic actions to save complete strangers to bring peace, to save life. I believe this is the true balance of the yin and the yang in action. It is the way

Chapter 1: January
JANUARY 8

The heart and soul

The heart simply knows how to work without much guidance from us. When we are fearful or excited, the heart works harder and puts undue pressure on itself; when we are at rest, exhausted or relaxed, the heart settles into its normal rhythm.

But what about the heart being our center of love? Can the ancient myth of Cupid and the heart representing love really be true? Can our heart bring love?

Science has found some interesting relevance worth knowing. Our thoughts actually inform our heart what is needed in terms of the mixture of nutrients in our blood to serve us best in the next moment. If we believe we are in fear, the heart will race and make us more alert, if we believe we are happy and rested, the heart will rest and fall into a welcome rhythm. The heart reacts to what we believe is truth just as much as the real experience we may incur.

So, this is where the saying "change your thoughts and you can change your life"

5

comes from.

We can think our way into a better place. If we could think positively through all situations, think with a mindset of abundance and love, our heart will make it so in our bodies. We will be happier and more in love in truth. Cupid apparently had it right!

Chapter 1: January
JANUARY 9

Inner voices!

Our inner voice is often the opening into your spirit. Many times in our daily routine, our inner voice beckons.

Each time you hear that soft inner voice what do you do? Most people hesitate to listen and often filter the voice through their own egoic questioning. So often we unknowingly silence our inner voice.

So, what to do?   If we can become aware of that hesitation to listen to our inner voice, we can ask ourselves if the God within us may be calling us to grow and is challenging us to do something bigger.

We will know if the voice is calling us to something greater in spirit. Next time, jump at the chance to risk growth, listen and take some chances.

Chapter 1: January
JANUARY 10

Are we us? How do we know?

Do you know who you really are? In spiritual growth circles you hear this question often, Who am I?

To get at the answer to "who am I" is difficult, I wonder why that is?

In most cases, to get deeper into the answer of who you really are, we need to "unlearn" much of what we have learned that actually hides our true self. So, what do we need to unlearn to find our true selves?

In knowing thy self, we need to unlearn the aspects of our self that we sometimes call ego. This is difficult to be sure because for many of us the ego has grown to protect us from harm or fear and the ego is who we think we are most of the time. The secret of unlearning is to chop away at the ego's assumptions, the roles we think we play and the actions we take. In the end, after chopping away, what is left is you.

Chapter 1: January
JANUARY 11

Is this for me?

My grandson always first believes every package is for him! That is perhaps not so bad a thought? What gift is awaiting us today? Will it be fleeting, so slight that if we are not centered we miss it or does it come crashing through our lives like a storm?

Embrace the day and its moments as a gift that was mailed to your door. It is happening whether we are aware or not, so why not be aware? From your awakening to your sleeping, gifts are present, but they often pass us as if we run a parallel life.

Morning has broken - like the first morning – black bird has spoken like the first bird. For every day it is always a new creation, always a gift for you to unwrap.

Chapter 1: January
JANUARY 12

How do you see?

I now revel in trying to see more than I see. When we begin to see with more than our eyes, the whole becomes clearer.   I heard about seeing with your heart yesterday and that is fundamentally what I mean by seeing more clearly.

Seeing with a touch or smell or intuition creates a clarity similar to waiting in the dark until your eyes adjust. It all becomes clear from nothing and comes into greater focus. There is so much more to see than our eyes allow! Take a step back, let the light adjust your focus and see more clearly.

Chapter 1: January
JANUARY 13

Do your thoughts guide you?

When we travel we often seek a professional guide to shed insights on what we are seeing. In our daily life, we do no such thing.

Our own thoughts guide most of us through our days. That is a scary thought, and let me tell you why. Most of our suffering says Buddha is caused by our thoughts! Thoughts have so much power over us and we are so consumed by them, that we miss the gifts all around us that would lead to a simpler more fulfilled life.

If we could set aside our constant thoughts and judgments and approach each moment as a gift we would be on the right track. If we sort a guide through each day we would be challenged more to see things from a new perspective.

Staying with the moment unwraps that gift as if you have a guide sitting by your side – and it then takes on a new light and shifts our premise from fear to love and from pain to hope.

Our thoughts often have no absolute truth and they only hold us hostage to our own worst worries and fears. We are better without believing them and stronger when we see who we become without them.

So seek the truth even from yourself. Test your own thoughts as to their reality, are they really true or a judgment or speculation? Let them go and enjoy what gift sits before you.

Chapter 1: January
JANUARY 14

This too shall pass!

This time honored gift to deal with life's pains has a darker side we often forget about. All great and joyous things will pass too!

What to do?

If this is true which all evidence of our senses support, we need to accept "what is" as a first step. When we begin to think at this level, the good and bad are the same.

Every experience helps us grow and is a gift, sometimes it's easy to see, and sometimes it feels impossible. However, in all times if we treat all imposters the same, we will find more truth and more peace as we let go.

Chapter 1: January
JANUARY 15

From what perspective do you come?

If we are looking at the universe and the grandeur of that expanse, does not your wonder overwhelm everything else?

Sometimes when we are looking at our own pain we see that as expansive too and we make it bigger than it really is. We create a helplessness.

In viewing our own pain, we need to sometimes pull back and look at it from a larger perspective, sort of seeing the greater picture from above. In doing so, you can more likely see the problem is not a barrier but something you can walk around or wait out.

Seek first the larger expanse and put all things in perspective, and then, all will be given you.

Chapter 1: January
JANUARY 16

What is your spirit telling you?

In nature, we see the wonders of universal law at work.
Trees know to breathe our exhaust, carbon dioxide, and give us back our life force oxygen. Birds know to fly and prepare for the seasons.

Creatures live their promise and play their part every day without over thinking their role. Our human mind has gotten in the way of what we know as a being.

Our spirit has the capacity to live in another world accessed by universal laws that somehow we think doesn't apply to us.

If we accept we are God's creatures, our first pure thoughts are likely from our spirit, sort of like our fellow creatures on this earth. Somewhere after that pure thought arrives, humans filter them with what we believe is higher intelligence and reasoning!

Over time, we have come to believe that filtering is an advancement of the human being and the answer is sometimes that is true, and sometimes it is not.

We need to remember that humans also over think and the development of our egos have created a filter inside our selves that bypasses reasoning. So, before displacing that Godly thought in favor of another, examine if it might be coming from a place of love, does it uplift us or others, is it seeking to slow us down to the moment at hand and if so, pay attention!

JANUARY 17

Are you a compassionate being?

Do you have an internal monitor that assures you of who you are? Often we are playing roles that others see. We mistake compassion with what we believe best for someone else but it really is feeding us. We give without shedding our judgment.

You have more to give... Just be and know you are worthy!

Chapter 1: January
JANUARY 18

Do your failings stop you from being?

Fears often stop us from trying, is that helpful? How do you feel about failing itself or getting stung for trying? Both of these help us grow so much more than doing nothing or even doing everything right!

Do you shudder and shake in fear of being wrong? Do you go back to where you were safe?

There is no better way to grow than to be stung for trying. Staying stagnant misses the point of being. We need to try, to help others, to step out and do something for the greater good.

Failure is our best teacher.

Chapter 1: January
JANUARY 19

Un-clutter your mind and slow down

Is your mind full? We don't need to clutter our minds with even more stuff, as we are too full now. Clutter always hides what is really there.

Be still more often and empty your mind. When you go slow enough you will not miss anything.

Chapter 1: January
JANUARY 20

Are you happy with everything?

If you can be pleased with every moment - you will find pleasure in the smallest of things. If you find pleasure in the smallest of things, you will be happy!

Chapter 1: January
JANUARY 21

Energy flows amongst all things

It is proven in quantum physics that all previously believed particles are really energy (frequencies) and mysteriously Einstein found that they can actually behave independently as if they learned from his experiments.

Thoughts are energy too and as we have discussed already, thoughts are also the cause of all effects in our lives. We are what we think after all. If we think positively we can gather that energy for good.

Finding the good in all bad is one way to see this energy transfer working. If a bad thing happens, if we can find the good in it or have faith that we can learn from this and become stronger - does it not work? Our expectations create results just like Einstein found in his experiments with particles.

We can create what we think!

Another view of this energy phenomenon is to think that there is no good or bad - - just how we perceive them or "think" they are! Ponder this for a moment.

If everything that happens just happens and the way we perceive it defines it, have we found the secret of happiness? Do our expectations make it so, like the discovery of quantum physics?

In this is a truth.

Chapter 1: January
JANUARY 22

Is there one interconnected universe?

Can you recall a time when you were thinking of someone and they called you or they wrote you a letter? Or you had a déjà vu experience where you felt you lived that moment before? These are signs of our connectedness and they are very common in our human experience!

We can't refute it and we can't explain it. Imagine a future time when we can harness that interconnected energy in every moment and build up each other through kind thoughts, through sincere prayer and with a knowing that when we lift others we lift ourselves!

That time is of course available in the now, we are just awakening into it!

Chapter 1: January
JANUARY 23

Are we heard?

Communication is a two way street and with all the noise in our lives, successfully communicating is a miracle.

The concept of deep listening is a pre-cursor to real communication. Until we can listen without judgment and without a pre-disposition we ourselves cannot influence communication.

Once we do, we still need a partner who does the same thing to receive the message. Before that occurs, their ego will take its best shot at interpreting, judging, pushing and twisting our intention!

However, if we come from a position of deep listening, our communication stays at the door of their soul, and when the door to their soul opens, light will flood through from those memories. It is then they will hear!

Chapter 1: January
JANUARY 24

Literally everything is a miracle!

Einstein had it right when he coined this phrase. Think about it? Bring wonder to your moments and the miracles are opened for you in every thing!

In our breathing, swallowing, thinking we see miracles. In the wonder of birds, flowers, spring we see miracles. In the expansiveness of the universe and of our own 'in-averse' we are miracles. Yes we are all parts of a miracle, how special are we!

Chapter 1: January
JANUARY25

Do you love....yourself?

Oh what a difficult question. Who am I? Am I lovable? All our human and egoic frailties rise up to meet us when we consider these questions. Some of us just can't love ourselves.

I believe that chasm of love for our self can be overcome a bit when we see ourselves as one with all things.

When we are the same as the tree, the wave, the note, or the molecule, then we see our part in the grand miracle of the universe, our loneliness goes away in favor of being part of a bigger plan.

In that knowing, we are all humbled, then we are more real even to ourselves, then we know only love. So, if we are part of the whole of everything, what is it to love another or ourselves when there are no longer any differences, no longer better or worse, no longer just me against the rest?

JANUARY 26

Are we "kind" by nature?

This is a truth when we are linked with our spiritual inner selves. We see it in crises; people flock to each other, help others often at the risk of themselves...why?

In crises, I believe our ego's are subordinated to our spirit. We live in the moment doing what we are most called to do and the direction is one of the spirit calling us to good. Our true selves, our kind souls emerge for the good of all!

This is proof of our innate kindness.

Chapter 1: January
JANUARY 27

Do we expose our truths in vulnerability?

When we are vulnerable, open to be seen as our true self, when we can open our hearts and stand in awe and wonder, then we are most connected to our spirit.

In these moments, we are humbled, vulnerable and most open to our truth. In these moments we are.

JANUARY 28

Do we hide our true self or is it being hidden?

This question tries to explain why we have so many layers of ego, roles, masks that hide our true selves. It makes no logical sense to me.

Why would we hide our spirit, our path directly to God? Then, if that logic is right, our true self must be hidden!

So, who is doing the hiding?

JANUARY 29

Are we in the middle?

Whatever we do, it seems compromise is the best place to be if you want progress particularly when dealing with humans of so many points of view. The government seems to work like that or at least tries to work like that.

I don't believe this works for the spirit in the same way. When ego is stripped, is there a middle way that is better than "the way"? Can the spirit find fulfillment in any way?   Does compromise to move forward not exist in the spirit world?

Not knowing is a good thing.

JANUARY 30

Is there more beauty inside beauty?

Many years ago I had the pleasure of sitting in an empty concert hall where the San Francisco orchestra was rehearsing for the gala reopening of the hall. There was one man sitting in the back of the orchestra section with the total composition in front of him.

The conductor led the orchestra through a beautiful piece, which to me was perfect and beautiful! Then at the conclusion of the piece, the conductor turned to the gentleman in the back and asked "did you think the violas came in too light at a particular point in this piece".

He turns the pages to find his notes and agrees...they make that change and this process occurs through many pages. I was impressed by the quality of the 'ear' and the extent of the memory of both the conductor and his assistant. They recalled not only the particular measure in the composition but the instrument that created an issue.

In the beauty, he found more beauty was possible!

It strikes me now that within each moment there must be a sacred moment that waits our uncovering! It is only when we can live within those smaller moments do we live fully and optimize our own composition! It is there we find more beauty inside beauty.

Chapter 1: January
JANUARY 31

Do you know the way?

There are natural cycles that repeat everywhere. The seasons show a springing forth, growing, pulling back and dying only to be born again. Flowers, seeds, trees do the same. The water cycle of rain, gather, evaporate, condense and rain again does the same.

So it is with us. God has shown the way. Even in the smallest things like breathing. We breath in, oxygen flows life through us, is processed and exhaled.

The way is not necessarily a distinct journey as our minds would have us believe, but stillness in subordination to our God...To just be!

Chapter 2: February
FEBRUARY 1

Slow down, you move too fast!

I have been told this line my whole adult life and it is true although I sense decreasingly so. My wife would not necessarily agree with that.

Here is a scientific truth around time and speed. Time slows with the increase of speed. Einstein conjectured that over the speed of light or whatever our infinite measure of speed is, time stands still!

Whomever we believe is our God, we all likely would agree that He/She works through the infinite speed associated with light, energy or thought.

So if God is at that level, time does not exist as we know it and in fact it stands still in that relationship. So to be with God we need to slow our pace, be in the moment, just be still...don't these all point to the same truth?

Slow down, you move too fast!

Chapter 2: February
FEBRUARY 2

Co - dependence?

I have experienced wonder in God's creations.

I have witnessed or read about remarkable miracles that showed me that we as part of God's creation also create.

Here are some examples that point me to consider more than I could ever know about creation and our part in that:

The mighty Sequoia communicates. I learned how trauma for one tree (a disease or fire) was experienced by all the other trees around it, and in a sense they communicated to others to prepare and protect themselves in some way!

Recent genetic experiments where heart cells placed together, start to share certain characteristics of that sharing, even to the point where two heart cells tend to create a third and distinctive heartbeat!

It is this miraculous dependence that demonstrates unmistakably to me that there is a oneness with the universe! I can extrapolate that dependency to every human interaction. We are brought together thousands of times per day as part of life.

When we are intentional in that interaction and place great value on the now moment, we create a co-dependence that is fulfilling God's purpose.

We act in oneness and as a result we co-create the holy and sacred next moment. We become part of creation.

Chapter 2: February
FEBRUARY 3

When do you really 'know' anything?

There are converging data points in brain science that is astounding and offer up more opportunity to be comfortable with not knowing when it comes to the mystical.

In using MRI brain scanning as part of science experiments, scientists have found that seconds before we choose a so-called random choice, the brain knows our choice!

So, I ask this question. Who is that inside us that really knows before our conscious does? Who is guiding our path to that depth that our conscious mind does not perceive the interventions?

When do we really know? And the deeper question is who specifically is we?

Chapter 2: February
FEBRUARY 4

Your inner doors!

Our evolution as human beings has included a theological perspective that we are changing our view of the same God as we go through inner doors of our species and become more aware and more enlightened!

Greater knowledge, consciousness and insights bring us closer to knowing the true God that dwells within.

We as individuals are of course on this same path. We need to walk through our own inner doors that are holding us back from seeing the God that lives within us!

Our soul knows only the truth and it is that we seek!

Chapter 2: February
FEBRUARY 5

Do you think too much?

Our normal human behavior is to use our brains to solve problems, even those problems that don't need thinking.

Consider this paradox I picked up from the Course in Miracles; each thought we have creates an effect, and as each thought also contains a judgment or an attachment, we most often work to resolve an effect that is created by us in thought!

In that case, we are resolving a problem that we in fact created!

If you can change your thoughts away from judging and attaching you will find great peace. We do think too much.

Chapter 2: February
FEBRUARY 6

Listen to the stream!

I am going to paraphrase a great parable from the Buddhist tradition. "Master - how do I achieve enlightenment?". Listen to the stream that sits in the forest was the answer. So the student listened and listened and finally heard the stream...he returned to the master who said " enter from there!". After many days of reflection the student returned, " Master, what if I could not hear that stream?". The master said " you would enter from there!"

Our finding of deeper truth comes from anywhere. We need to come from a place of stillness and deep reflection. In being still, we can listen for that stream and find truth from there, whether or not we actually hear the stream, whether or not there is a stream!

Chapter 2: February
FEBRUARY 7

Sharing?

Here is a controversial point of view on sharing. It is like a chameleon, its colors can change based on intent. It is not always good.

In concept, we can share sadness and divide it, while sharing joy expands it?

While sharing is the same, the affects of that sharing can differ quite a bit based on our intention. In sharing joy we expand the universe and create more joy. This is like an idea, when an idea is shared the idea to grows because many people now have that idea and can build upon it, sharing joy does the same thing.

In sadness though, our intent to share is sometimes selfish. We often look to others to hold our pain or take it from us and many times that burden is too great for another to hold.

We can however, adjust our intent when sad to assure we expand the goodness! Look to move through the pain and share to divide versus shift the pain. Dividing pain frees our souls and makes the yoke light for all of us.

Chapter 2: February
FEBRUARY 8

Are you satiated?

Our grandson picked up on that word early...it was adorable to hear the little guy say I am satiated. But hearing it over and over struck a chord relevant to satiability in our lives.

Are we never satisfied?

The wanting of something we don't have, the attachment to things we do have is a battle we can't win easily! To be truly satiated, we must let go of attachments and let go of judgments at the same time. We must live in the moment the spirit gives us, free of attachment.

To be satiated is a gift of the spirit...may you be satiated!

Chapter 2: February
February 9

Walls

Often we build walls to protect us, safe inside the walls keeping others out and keeping us 'in'! Our inside walls take years to build. They are invisible to us; full of things like attachments, memories, roles we play, self worth, dreams.

Our walls are our ego's, built to protect the self we created by saving all that past stuff. The true self resides behind that wall and to break through, the wall needs to be penetrated or taken down or climbed over.

We can't get to truth without dismantling our ego in some way and finding our spirit huddled inside.

Chapter 2: February
February 10

How much of you do you know?

Our ego is like the wall that is tall and strong and safe. It has taken us a lifetime to build and we consider it us, right? We play a role that we identify as us! We see ourselves in certain ways informed by our experience, we can state some special characteristics of ourselves, attributes, talents, prize possessions that define us.

Is that really you or a creation of your ego? I don't think many of us really know because the wall is too big!

Chapter 2: February
February 11

Simple is best

We are far from simple, in fact we are immeasurably complex.

So how do we get from the complex here to simple there? Lao Tzu, the Chinese sage that came along around Buddhas time said that simplicity is one of only three things to teach.

He teaches to find simplicity in nature. He looks for wisdom in the universal nature of all things and he follows that path.

The secret around this is to recognize the truth of 'what is' in this moment, not what we would like it to be and then accept it as is.

Stay simple. What is – really is.

Chapter 2: February
FEBRUARY 12

Afternoon tea!

I started drinking tea a few years ago. At first it was to quell the stomach upset of too much coffee, but it quickly became a ritual. I enjoy earl grey for the experience it brings. Tea is a marvelous metaphor for life. We take leaves from a plant, dry them, and then steep them in a ritual of hot water, time and patience. When the fragrance and time is right, we sit in expectations of gratitude, sip slowly to nurture ourselves and enjoy.

We can learn from the tea process. Like the tea leaves, we begin fresh and fragrant, we steep ourselves in hot water again and again until we feel like we have given all we can.

We learn to be patient and we nurture the process of steeping through the hot water. When we have steeped enough, we are ready and then we sit in quiet, we feel the warmth versus the heat, we are energized by the fragrance, and with every slow sip, we let gratitude flow through us, warming us all over.

We begin again.

Chapter 2: February
FEBRUARY 13

Seeing wonder

I stand in awe much more often these days. I can see so much I never saw before. Almost like the saying "I see it again for the first time".

With Gods eyes, wonder is in everything and I strive to go there.

I have been fortunate to see and feel wonder in daily things at times, and sometimes I see things I have looked at hundreds of times but missed. To see with Gods' eyes are a gift that we can nurture like putting on a pair of glasses to see more clearly.

Love as expressed in wonder is everywhere; to the left of and to the right, above us and below us, in front and in back - inside us!

Chapter 2: February
FEBRUARY 14

Express yourself!

I watched a powerful Oprah interview with Lady Gaga. She is touching a nerve in many that they are ok where they are and with whom they are...born like this - as she sings.

Amongst her wild expressions, multi personalities and extreme showmanship, she is helping people express who they are and to feel good about it. She has likely saved lives. It seems that our society has suppressed expression of the true self in favor of some odd ego game around conforming. This is dangerous as through suppression we build walls of hurt. Gaga is giving voice to authenticity...that can only be good.

If her intentions are positive this is a consciousness arising!

FEBRUARY 15

Anti-bodies and immune systems.

A new study suggests quite logically that our over protectiveness of our children is not protecting them. It seems our diligence in keeping our kids clean and away from potential risks in the world has backfired. The study says that preventing our kids from playing with dirt, and exposing them to germs has diminished their immune systems.

This is an interesting message about living fully. Only when we face the germs openly do we diminish their ability to harm us. In all things, facing the evil, delivers us a more fulfilling tomorrow.

FEBRUARY 16

What defines your day?

Everyday, there are miracles and misery surrounding us.

We are all gifted the ability to 'see' moments of glory that surround us and decide to spend our time in those moments rather than misery. When we can do that, we can feel peace.

Yet, it just takes one small otherwise unimportant thought or event for me and I am torn away from that peace and immersed in the misery; worried about what happens next and my humanness is exposed.

That often-unimportant thought disrupts my peace and makes no sense in the larger picture. So why do we give such insignificance the power to pull us from glory?

What defines your day, the Miracle or the misery?

FEBRUARY 17

Light and dark

I am curious about the theological significance of light because it is used so often. I have heard a few different levels of understanding, one is that darkness can not stand up to light and in fact it is the absence of light that creates darkness.

Another is that light overcomes darkness, so in essence light overwhelms dark and brings light.

These both offer much truth and deep perspective.

Which is it for you? Are you light unaware that darkness even exists or are you in the dark looking for a light to see?

Chapter 2: February
FEBRUARY 18

How long is your resume?

We often define ourselves by our list of accomplishments. We feel in some way more complete and worthy with a long list - the longer the better, right?

All too often, we cannot see the person behind those accomplishments and having a longer list sometimes hides the person more.

The focus on achieving takes us away from seeing the miracles in the journey.

The next time you read or prepare a resume, give some time to find out the journey to get there. It will tell you much more about yourself and the author, their life and their soul.

Chapter 2: February
FEBRUARY 19

Glass blowing

We sat at a glass blowing exhibit and watched the making of a vase. What was noteworthy to me was that the glass hardened to be unworkable so quickly. Time and again, it was back in the oven firing again as it needed heat to allow it to be reformed or changed without breaking.

We are like glass. We harden so quickly that we become immune to change and cannot reform ourselves without breaking. What a lesson to reflect upon.

If we keep ourselves malleable so that we can more easily form and reform, we will avoid becoming so hard that we need to break to change.

Nicodemus

"Can we be born again? Re-enter the womb?" Nicodemus was a Jewish scholar and yet curious and open enough to seek time with Jesus to find the truth in his words.

Jesus was patient with Nicodemus in answering this question, yet I believe the question itself seems incongruent with a man of Nicodemus's stature and education. Why is the story written this way?

Is born again so difficult a metaphor that Nicodemus would be confused?

A new born has certain characteristics common to being one with God. They are fully dependent and have to be trusting. They are free of judgment and attachment. They know not of reason and do not have a stream of constant mind chatter driving their thoughts. They trust and feel love from those that share it with them. Yet his questions were about the womb?

It tells me that the best of us get caught up in our own thoughts and egos. Unlearning that for the learned is harder because there is more to unlearn.

Perhaps Nicodemus may have been right - being born again is hard work! We may as well compare it to going back into the womb.

Tuning up!

Have you ever listened to an orchestra tuning up and then voila the glory of the music comes? That is a neat experience.

I see our lives as likened to that tune up. There are many different inner and outer voices swirling around us, each trying to find the right pitch, sounding like a group of pre-K children making noise.

Each recognition of the right pitch from those among us, slowly diminishes the noise yet leaving others the time to find their pitch. Then voila, the music begins and we hear its beauty.

FEBRUARY 22

When one hesitates, one is lost!

This popular cliché' has a spiritual sense, hesitation in hearing the inner voice knocking and not taking action can put us in a place where we feel lost. In all these times of hesitation, we miss the moment God intended for us to experience.

Give your inner voice more power and avoid being lost and like an old friend, more of the joys good friends bring will come to you.

Chapter 2: February
FEBRUARY 23

Urgent pre-intent

Is there really an urgency to make some of the decisions we do? Often when we are burdened with a decision we can't wait to make, waiting is the answer.

Somehow tomorrow always adds clarity to the urgent matters of yesterday. When forced into urgency, revert to your soul for guidance, breathe in - pause – breathe out. Let the issues in, ponder, let them out. Tomorrow comes with a new clarity.

Chapter 2: February
FEBRUARY 24

Who do we feed?

One Native American folk tale exists where the elder tells the child of the boy who struggles with the good wolf and the bad wolf in his mind. The child asks, but which wolf will win? The one you feed the elder says.

In like fashion, we need to choose to feed our true or false self. The one watching, the one still, that one!

Chapter 2: February
FEBRUARY 25

Travelling through life.

If you are on the move can you ever experience life? I recently drove 1400 miles from NY to Florida. I drove past a lot, often taking in the billboards planted for me to see. I have been thinking about those billboards and equating them to pointers we pass while on the run each day.

What is behind the billboards? We miss the life that is there; the small towns, meaningful conversations, beautiful fields and flowers, and the local people.

As we run on the highways of our life's work, we would benefit by slowing down, getting off the highway enough to 'see' and 'touch' and 'feel' life before moving on.

Life exists in the little moments behind the billboards!

Chapter 2: February
FEBRUARY 26

Who's to say?

What makes me right? There are 6 billion people on earth...most following different religions with different doctrines. I have learned there are fundamental truths similar in all of them and therefore I choose to lean toward tolerance and truth versus doctrine. I know I don't know.

Chapter 2: February
FEBRUARY 28

The stones of cranberry rapids

We have dear friends who have a Godly place in the Adirondack mountains. . They were telling us on our last visit about moving stones in the river bed to redirect the flow of their river.

I wondered about how all of us need to occasionally lift our pant legs, get in the river of our souls and unclog the flow by moving those stones out of the way. Some stones are easy to move - some need dear friends to help lift and carry. When the intended work is done, our spirit flows naturally.

Chapter 2: February
FEBRUARY 29

Beauty is truth, truth beauty

John Keats dying at the age of 24 wrote these words. "Beauty in whatever form we can appreciate is truth and has truth contained within it....but true beauty seems to make it 'one' by its simplicity."

When faced with understanding the deepest meaning of life from his deathbed, Keats saw a beauty that overcame all darkness, and in that beauty he could not differentiate the joy. He was one with spirit.

Chapter 3: March
MARCH 1

Is that so?

Elkhart Tolle tells a story of a Zen master who was accused by a neighbor girl of being the father of her baby, so that she did not expose her relations with a boy friend. The parents of the girl confronted the master...he answered 'is that so'. Then when the child was born, they forced him to take the child and care for it as his responsibility...he responded 'is that so' and took the baby and cared for it as his own...then a year later the daughter confessed the truth, the parents went to the master and deeply apologized and took the baby back...'is that so' the master said.

In all things that confront us, we need to accept what is before we unwrap the underlying gift. In doing so, we will always know joy!

Chapter 3: March
MARCH 2

Does multi-tasking create a failure of spirit?

What is thought to be a key and valued attribute in our society could be getting in the way of joy rather than creating it! Multi-tasking at its core is 'busy ness' and that always subverts joy. We are called by our spirit to be still yet our world around us calls us to be as busy as we can.

We cannot live well in that conflict. Try to take one task, one moment at a time and you will see the difference.

Chapter 3: March
MARCH 3

Saving our species

God's creatures save out of a natural law, enabling them to survive and evolve. The squirrel finds and saves their nuts as food for instance and their genetic code allows them to repeat and survive as a species.

Humans in the developed world are different in that we have evolved past the physical necessities of other of God's creatures. Our 'saving' has moved more toward the spiritual. With each step we take toward finding our true selves and the power of our souls, we imprint on our genetic code for future humanity the plan of survival.

Our evolution is tied to our spiritual progress; finding the spirit within, recognizing our Oneness as a species makes us more likely to survive.

Chapter 3: March
MARCH 4

Do we fully digest our moments?

One thing about digestion is that it takes a lot of time and consumes a lot of energy. Our natural behavior will be to slow down and focus on the digestion.

When we experience a Moment that requires deeper reflection do we take that time to stop and digest it properly?

If we don't take that time and move on to the next moment, we risk indigestion. That indigestion will create unrest because we will not be able to associate the feeling engendered by that moment to the right moment and we risk not reconciling.

We need to digest every moment before moving on.

Chapter 3: March
MARCH 5

From where do we draw super human strength?

I remember an altercation in my life that involved physical harm. My wife fought the man off of me who was half again larger than me! That normally could not happen was it not for the super strength of that moment protecting a loved one!

Our loved one, a treasured friend, a child or grandchild, all provoke that ability to do super hero things. Why? This super strength comes from our natural selves...it is a place that we can all go to lift ourselves to new heights!

We have all heard the line that we only use a small percent of our brain. It is that space we can go to draw strength any time. It is our spirit space. As we find ways to intentionally go there, we will grow miraculously!

Chapter 3: March
MARCH 6

Are memories real?

When faced with this moment, what role does memory play and how is it created and nurtured for us to benefit most?   Is it real in a sense that we remember it or is it how we remember that becomes real?

The power of now is manifest in being available at the moment for the moment. This requires no other baggage to come along including memories.

Memories are likely created by ourselves to make sense of the moments that passed and some may have not been adequately reconciled. Believing this has some truth in it, we need to be careful about memories as our own thoughts and bias impact how we remember, how we judge and how we act.

Chapter 3: March
MARCH 7

To be or not to be?

Is it nobler not to be? To not make waves, to fit in, get along, to find your place among many, feel somewhat less than, to belong?

What is 'to be' then?   Let me offer a different thought.

"To be" is outside all the roles we find ourselves playing. It is the truth inside, It is the 'us' that watches us play those silly roles!. 'To be' is to forsake the ego in favor of the one true self, a gift of the spirit, holy!

To be is what we strive to become deep inside after we unwrap all those 'not to be' roles.

Chapter 3: March
MARCH 8

Do we give for us or for others?

Giving is a barometer of worth, and sometimes it becomes distorted expressions of our own self worth. We do that with compassion too. Even 'feeling' compassion for another can most times be a feeding of ourselves. "we are better in a way", however that gets distorted by the ego.

We saw this first hand when visiting the kakuma refugee camp in Kenya and refugees from Sudan. We arrived all set to show how compassionate we can be, and a funny thing happened. The refugees did not want nor need our compassion! The refugees wanted us to tell others of their plight, this was too big an issue for our compassion!

In an unexpressed way they had compassion for us. Lifting us up in their God, showing us that true joy of the spirit happens when you have no attachments, no things! There are no needs to express at that level.

There was nothing really lacking other than our knowing. We learned.

Chapter 3: March
MARCH 9

'What is?'

Seeing 'what is '- is a difficult task. Law enforcement needs to find clues from a scene of an accident often confused by witnesses' testimony rather than aided by that testimony, and unfold what really happened. Witnesses often see different things filtered by their own bias and life experience. So what do we really see?

 Our conscious mind sees what it wants to see through its own filter and therefore often does not see what truly is! This is the essence of the teaching around the Course in Miracles that all things are not as they seem or how we label them.

Here is a quick exercise:
Take a deep breath, close your eyes, be still. Imagine no thing labeled. Imagine all things as they are, a tree is not a tree but a living breathing part of our world, a table is not hard and fabricated but actually has moving atomic elements inside, we are like them both, a part of the one. Imagine yourself as part of the one. That is 'what is' at the center of everything.

Chapter 3: March
MARCH 10

Stirring water.

Lao-Tzu tells a story about stirring water. He says knowledge creates troubles and using knowledge to fix them is like stirring water to make it clear.

The Course in Miracles tells us our thoughts are the cause of all effects and therefore all of our troubles. We cannot address our troubles by the very thing that created them, that's like letting the fox in the hen house!

We must stop the thinking and be still. In stillness we can see that without that thought, the trouble lightens, without that thought we are happier, without that thought we move forward! If the thought is not the absolute truth, where were we going with that anyway? We can let it go and cause no stress or even no harm.

Still water clears!

Chapter 3: March
MARCH 11

Resistance

Water flows the path of least resistance. When we resist, we fail to accept what is and invariably feed the very thing we resist. In many ways you become what you resist because of the energy placed upon that item.

When stressed with what is happening, Surrender, let go, be still. Then you release the flow to its least resistance and you will be more calm and capable to work with what is.

Chapter 3: March
MARCH 12

Sabbath.

Rest is the root of the word restorative. When the tumult of life hits us like the crashing of waves, it is rest that brings us home to our core. Our sabbath is essential to that and I fear the sabbath idea has been lost in today's pace of living.

Our creator understood our needs for rest and through prophets we came to understand the day of rest as holy. We need to touch those holy places that restore us and in today's world that means with more intention. We need to sabbath routinely, as often as we work, within our work, around our work.

Finding the sabbath in a moment rather than a day; in quiet, in prayer, in gratefulness, in wonder. Just a moment of reflection will replenish our souls. With a replenished soul, we are ready for anything!

Chapter 3: March
MARCH 13

Faith has a second chance!

One thing has always struck me about the Peter and Jesus bible story about walking on water. In this well-known story, Peter's demonstration of faith was to get out of the boat and walk toward Jesus on the water. That is faith!

He then is perceived to have lost faith when he fell into the water because Jesus called him a man of little faith.

What we often miss in the story is that Peter had a second chance that we all come across in life. When we fall particularly after showing deep faith in an outcome that failed to appear, we panic and flail about because we see our faith crumbling about us. It is at that lowest time, that real faith reveals! In a surrendering, in letting go, accepting what is, we bring real faith to our soul and we can move through any circumstance. If we flail and panic like Peter, we sink. Peter missed his chance to reveal real faith in the face of despair and panic, and that was what Jesus called to our attention!

Chapter 3: March
MARCH 14

Are we part of the universe or bystanders?

Humans use our gift of reason and intellect to try and understand the universe as if we are apart from it. It turns out that in the science we find miracles and perhaps in a paradoxical way we are discovering ourselves in that science!

Our genetic makeup, cell structures, the flow of nutrients, breathing, thought processing, senses, and unknown as yet capabilities are all reflections of the greater universe in which we belong. We are in fact the universe in microcosm.

Instead of finding ourselves in everything, we would do well also to find everything in ourselves.

Chapter 3: March

MARCH 15

Are we there yet?

Funny memories come to mind when thinking of kids who wish to rush the journey to get 'there'.

How often do we do the same thing in a less irritating fashion? We often look past the rewards of being in the moment in favor of looking for what is 'over there', what is next.

The reality is there is never 'over there' because when we get there, it is always 'here!'

Chapter 3: March
MARCH 16

I am bored!

How often do we feel bored? When I reflect on just that, I ask how could anyone be bored? Is there nothing to do, read, imagine, think about?

At it's core, boredom is about a hole inside. We feel shallow or wanting, we desire, we have longing but we can't label it as such, so we label it bored! To escape boredom we must fill the emptiness, feel the essence of life around us and raise our consciousness of all things natural. Then, awe and wonder fill our thoughts and we can have no concept of boredom.

Chapter 3: March
MARCH 17

Friction is good!

We often struggle to keep the friction of life to a minimum, like protecting our loved ones from pain. Yet, It is often that same friction that takes our spirit and burns a sparkling diamond! We are in need of friction to grow. We are a stone waiting to be formed, smoothed, and shined up for all eternity by our creator - so for God's sake let there be friction.

Chapter 3: March
MARCH 18

IOU's?

Each of Gods creatures knows and fulfills it's purpose as a matter of instinct. They exist in an innate knowing. Why is this so hard for us?

We search for purpose because we do not exist in knowing, we think we know better and some of us think we know everything. I believe we think too much.

Our thoughts bring us to other places away from our instinct. We worry about where we are going! We think incessantly of the future. We lose our purpose in thought. Our soul's purpose is here and present waiting for us to be there too. It doesn't take IOU's either, so lost moments are lost!

Chapter 3: March
MARCH 19

Dark holes.

Light consumes dark and dark cannot exist in its presence. Dark holes in the universe work counter to that! I was reading about these heated and dark areas on the ocean floor where nothing was presumed to grow or live...nothing! Once scientists and technology could overcome the pressure to explore those dark, deep areas of the ocean, they found that there is a plethora of growth, of living, of vibrancy!

Even in our darkest places of despair when all logical hope is gone, there is a light that can't be seen. When we are suffering, there is still love, still peace. When we are at war, still hope; and when in despair light surrounds us and upholds us despite the darkness we see. We don't lose "truth" because it is not visible to us!

So it is.

Chapter 3: March
MARCH 20

Cutting a path to our soul

Ever consider the pioneers cutting a new path out west through the wild? What strength, fortitude, perseverance, and spirit they had! A journey into our soul requires that same set of attributes.

Lifted by a desire for a new life, we, like pioneers swing the proverbial blade through the brush of our mind to cut a new path! We cut brush that covered our inner self for years...little by little exposing a path to pursue and some of our inner beauty. Then after much work, forests become meadows, and we find a clearing that is peaceful and a place to rest. We can pitch a tent and stay for awhile!

Chapter 3: March
MARCH 21

Feeling?

Feelings are believed to come from deep inside us, a reflection of how our true self reacts to the moment! Could feelings be false? I think we need to be open to that. The ego can distort feelings by calling up memories or worries from the past.

When we are overcome with emotion we need to take a deep breath and allow our soul to engage. More often than not, the truth lives somewhere else.

Chapter 3: March
MARCH 22

Hot charcoal

There is a spiritual proverb that says that holding anger is like picking up a hot charcoal to throw at someone in anger - it only burns you! Let go of the anger and you will be free.

There is another side of that story that often is overlooked....don't even pick up the hot charcoal or anger in the first place. When faced with a reason to be angry, be still, open your mind and let the reason float right by you, losing power with each passing moment. When it passes off beyond your grasp, You will be more free!

Chapter 3: March
MARCH 23

Metaphorically letting go!

There is a movement in qi gong that reflects the human story of holding on. Ancient trapping methods for monkeys included putting rice in a coconut with an opening smaller than a monkey's fist. An open hand fits right in, but when the monkey closes their fist to grab the rice they can't get it out!

In their unwillingness to let go, they are stuck attached to the coconut and they get caught. The qi gong movement plays this out, metaphorically letting go and at the same time being free.

We don't need the rice - let go!

Chapter 3: March
MARCH 24

Can you return to now?

This is an odd reflection on purpose. When we stray from the present moment, just where do we go?

Our thoughts project us like a time machine all over our humanity...we are off to the future making up stories and creating fears...or we are traveling back recreating memories in our minds....making some better and some worse.

Are we so afraid of this moment we can't stay awhile? If we let ourselves remain in the now, that future and past we worry about so much melts away and becomes now!

Now is a good place, we should return there!

Chapter 3: March
MARCH 25

The un-played purpose

We have a beautiful player piano that sits un-played. A dear friend played it recently and despite it sounding wonderful to me, he stopped and said 'oh boy, you need to get her tuned!'

Just a few months later I was reading in our great room quietly and I became consumed by the silence of the piano. I felt its sadness. The air held this energy of grief....I stopped reading and turned on its player mechanism...and we both enjoyed her sound. She was happy singing how she was made to sing (in or out of tune) and I reveled in her joy !

We are like that! We are all waiting to be heard, to share our gifts, to do what we were made to do...turn on your player, whether you are in tune or not, you were meant to play!

Chapter 3: March

MARCH 26

Singing, dancing, creating!

What is it about singing and dancing that lights up the soul? Much like being still enables us to hear the quiet vibrations of our soul, the creative process does the same thing.

Despite the noise created by singing or dancing, the creative process stops our mind from thinking incessantly and creates its own focused stillness. Any creative process does this same thing and commands our soul the same way!

What have you created today?

Chapter 3: March
MARCH 27

Power

I am not sure where power became such a gift to us humans. Our ego's push us to be above others, to feel stronger and better than, to grab more for ourselves. Our souls meanwhile minimize the ego and seek to take its power away.

These two ideas are powerful yet incongruous and only one can set you free.

Chapter 3: March
MARCH 28

Cycles

Have you considered how natural events are repetitive cycles? They go round and round or 'out and in' with a constancy that follows a universal law. For example, We breath out - stop - breath in; tides go out - stop - and come in; fall goes out - stops - and spring comes in. Are we not the same?

Eckhart Tolle says life has no opposite though? Deaths' opposite is birth. We physically come in at birth, stop and go out at death; life however precedes and proceeds both. If this is true, our souls must be part of a higher order cycle we have yet to discern.

Likened to the expansion of the universe, Our souls have much more to experience.

MARCH 29

The gift of shedding!

Snakes scare me. Why is it that from ancient times they have come to signify healing and rejuvenation! From Egypt to Greece the snake was a symbol of healing. It's shedding of skin was a symbol of rejuvenation and vitality. The medical insignia even has the snake as its primary symbol drawn from mythology.

So what is it about shedding that promotes healing? As spiritual beings we need to often shed our skin or we become victim to our own boundaries. With the courage to shed comes rejuvenation and new life and with new life comes healing.

MARCH 30

Human shedding!

We don't let go of things easily and as a result our growth is often painful. Oh if we could just shed our skin and emerge anew, with no thoughts of past horrors or worries of future shortcomings.

We can do that metaphorically but in reality our ego protects those walls we have built and brings fear anytime we think of changing, "what if we don't like the new person, what if we hurt someone else, what if we shed something good, what if we need that something tomorrow?"

It would be so much easier to just shed and move on !

MARCH 31

Stroke of insight!

Jill Bolte Taylor wrote of her 'living' through her stroke, that her exclusive time with her spiritual side of the brain gave her great insights. She could see and feel the energy from people around her, although she did not know how or why, she could understand people's intention and kindness without a word being said.

Therefore, first impressions are made long before we interact, and long before we engage another person. We need to bring intention to all our moments as underlying the trust in any interaction is what we bring to it.

That my friend is a stroke of insight!

Chapter 4: April
APRIL 1

Can we be real?

I struggle with this. So many including myself work hard to find the still place inside and If being real is our ultimate purpose should it not be easier?

We have so much clutter inside our minds, so many thoughts, roles, stories that have become who we know as 'us', the path to being real is full of land mines. Navigating the path and removing those land mines that clutter our paths is the journey we take.

Clutter has to go; and so it is.

Chapter 4: April
APRIL 2

Cocoons, a Holy wait!

In nature there is nothing more dramatic in terms of change than the caterpillar, working at the lowest level of ground crawling, then spinning their cocoon and emerging a butterfly, soaring at the highest heights.

There are so many truths uncovered in their example, among them our need for time to be still. Once a caterpillar spins the cocoon they sit in silence waiting. They do it with a 'knowing ' - a knowing faith and God does not let them down!

Our human cocoons work the same way; at points of major transformation, it is best to sit still in Holy wait. Seek nothing except Gods plan as it unfolds before us. Know that this will come and in time emerge a butterfly.

Chapter 4: April
APRIL 3

Rivers ramble

GPS machines are a great invention, helping us navigate around to places with more certainty. When you program your journey, the machine typically asks you to designate the fastest route, most use of highways, least use of highways. What if our GPS asked us if we wanted the route of least resistance, would we take it?

I can imagine our interest...is it faster? Does it avoid traffic delays? How does it know? I presume that route could not predict when you would arrive. It would be funny to see this in a candid camera routine, someone presses route of least resistance and it predicts an arrival time of 'unknown!'

I believe, safely so, that no one would take that path! In nature, Rivers ramble to the path of least resistance, going where they are intended. They are not on a schedule, they arrive when they arrive. At the end of their journey they form a great body of water and in their journey create a beautiful landscape.

That journey is our journey! We somehow need to find the courage to take that path of least resistance; it is our destiny...it may seem longer than we believe we can afford at any given moment, it may contain some uncertainty, but in the larger scheme of things, you will arrive when you are expected to arrive, you will be awakened by the smoothness of the journey and you create a beautiful landscape of a life in doing so!

Chapter 4: April
APRIL 4

Talking

Why two ears?
Our grandson is a talker! How often we say listen.

In creation we were meant to listen more, God not only gave us two ears but we have less resistance in listening as well. By resistance I mean that God also gave us the natural ability to speak less rather than hear less.

Ever think about how easy we can close our mouth versus close our ears? So, In creations grand design, we should listen more! In the quiet of listening, the real inner self has time to speak, we have time to listen, hear, respond.

We engage the spirit without saying a word!

Chapter 4: April
APRIL 5

Hurt and healing work together

Have you ever taken a walk in woods that are not tended by humans? It is an amazing place of grace. To the eye, at first glance it appears like chaos. Trees down, branches down everywhere! Upon closer exploration, clothed among that chaos is a distinguishable order! There is a spring of new life everywhere! New trees grow quickly from the nutrients of the fallen trees, nests are formed for birds, dens for animals. It goes on and on!

We can learn from that story! When we fall, we create the space that nurtures and feeds growth. Our pain and vulnerability serve as nutrients that open us to new directions, new growth and ultimately healing!

Like the trees, we need do nothing but lay in quiet faith. God's hand will create a distinguishable order out of chaos and create anew.

Chapter 4: April
APRIL 6

Seeds crack!

Jesus speaks of the seeds spread -those fallen on stone will not be able to grow and flourish....but those In soil or otherwise protected have a chance to flower!

Another part of the story that is untold is the fact the flowering seed also has to crack wide open. It is not enough to be a seed and be in soil; the invisible, yet Godly process of creation and evolution requires that seed to break itself wide open to grow.

We too need to break to grow. Our own shells have many layers, some are built by past barriers, others are created by being told we are not good enough, others even keep love away.

All must be broken wide open! It is then that we can follow the 'way' toward our own light and flourish!

Chapter 4: April
APRIL 7

Holy songs

In tribal cultures the medicine man or the healer are key members of the tribe. Often they look for signs of the pain in song!

The songs that come from the sick are voices of pain; moaning, coughing, humming, screaming! This works for me in that when we can give voice to our pain, healing comes sooner.

All voices of pain are holy songs! Our God listens for the songs that are Holy whether they are screams, prayer or the humming sound of desperation. We must give our pain voice for healing to come sooner. Sing your pain, it matters not that you label it...it matters only that you sing.

Chapter 4: April
APRIL 8

Being yourself

Do I care what others think?
I received a lesson of soul preservation when I was a youth that stays with me. Somehow my friends took sides in some unclear battle and I landed on the outside. It was a seminal moment in my life. How would it shape me? Would I lose self in response? Would I always be more impacted by what others think?

When I look back with the benefit of time and wisdom, God created the place where I could grow from that rather than suffer. With astute parenting, I was encouraged to tryout for a baseball team. Having never played organized ball, starting at 14 was a little scary...but I did. I made the team and from there created friends and memories and opened opportunities that I honor today.

The lesson I have taken is that we best find ourselves and our way on our own. Much is risked by waiting for others to tell us who they think we are and much is lost believing it!

Chapter 4: April
APRIL 9

Center of the "I"

Mark Nepo tells this story and makes this reflection. The center of the eye, the pupil is actually empty. In that emptiness, our entire world enters and becomes known to us! In a spiritual sense, the 'I' is the empty center where we can see everything by emptying all things.

When we can empty our self of the 'I" in us, it is then we find our true self so clearly visible, and we are satiated.

APRIL 10

Tomorrow is today disguised

Why put off till tomorrow what you can do today? I believe that was Wimpy in the old Popeye cartoons talking about hamburgers! In a spiritual sense that Wimpy was deep!

To our conscious mind, tomorrow never comes, so we potentially put off the action indefinitely! When we listen to that small voice telling us to put something off, we disconnect from the moment at hand.

If we choose to disconnect too many moments a strange thing happens. We lose intention and let life happen to us, we feel out of control, overwhelmed, we tend to no thing and create a loneliness! So, we need to see each thought of hesitation (that little voice saying do that tomorrow) as a gift of our inner self-saying 'pay attention', this moment needs you to really be here!

APRIL 11

Being spiritual

Organized religions are taking note of those among us who say they are not religious but spiritual. I view this trend as good and not bad! I see anything that brings one closer to God a good thing as religion began for that same reason and I believe was intended to bring all followers to the same place eventually. In this case of finding spirituality first, we are brought into the one God one universe concept and that we are all spirit filled beings without labeling.

Perhaps that makes more sense as a place to start to find our God and our true self.

APRIL 12

Use our roots to grow

Photosynthesis is a miracle that takes the energy of the sun and transforms that into nutrients for roots to grow stronger, feeding more growth. Have you ever given thought that roots grow away from light just as the flower grows towards it?

Yet they work together! In a strange way the light enables darkness to grow and there is even a symbiotic connection creating more light.

This metaphorically explains the strength we find in coming through pain or tragedy; where in retrospect we see our dark time had fed us and built the strength of our roots that enabled more growth, and the promise of more light and more strength in the end.

Chapter 4: April
APRIL 13

Giving voice to love

It is speaking that makes humans human. Each thought making its way through our filters, and out of our mouths is in fact a miracle!

Speaking makes us human. Even if we speak to 'no one', we still speak through to our soul! It is part of our fundamental being. It is what we do to free our spirit as humans just like worms crawling or birds flying. Speaking can break us out of our self made enclosures and reach deeper into our inner selves, connecting our humanness to our being! Speaking has us relate to each other and relate to God.

Speaking gives voice to love.

Chapter 4: April
APRIL 14

Water seeks its lowest point

Lao-Tzu compares our souls to water in that we are most content being humble.

He draws this conclusion relating that water seeks its lowest point always and is content resting as a great body of water.

The great oceans are the final resting grounds of rivers rambling across terrains from the tops of mountains, reaching the height of greatness when they are at their lowest, the point of greatest humility.

It is then we resist nothing and become part of the great ocean of which we are one!

Chapter 4: April

APRIL 15

Self-importance and the storms in our life

We were in Dublin when a priest told us an Irish folklore....'see that mountain to the west' he said, 'it is said that if you can't see the mountain, it is raining...if you can, it is going to rain!'.

I got to thinking about local weather and isolated systems that cause rain as metaphors for storms in our life. Many attach the cause for these storms to our own behaviors or failings? These are folklores we tell ourselves ? "I should have done this or that...if I only....I blame myself!". Our self importance or misplaced thoughts are the real storm, we do not have the power to impact the fury of the storm nor it's coming or going. We just are and that is okay.

Chapter 4: April
APRIL 16

My heart is sinking!

How many times has your heart sunk? That immediate feedback from our soul of loss is an amazing miracle. Those moments are like instant messaging from the God within!

Sometimes our need for grace is so large, that our inner truth lets you know loud and clear to stop and take note! When this occurs, we need to pay attention, embrace ourselves in the moment, and listen. It is God calling.

Chapter 4: April
APRIL 17

There's so much dust!

In the direct sunlight you can see dust particles swirl, rise and fall! I was reminded we are all dust and to dust we shall return, so in that moment I gave those dust particles the reverence they deserved.

Can our attention to the smallest things actually be Holy? If we can seek truth or God in the smallest item nearest us, we are likely to become more at peace.

So when you are impacted by the sadness or pain of the moment, focus your attention on the holiness of the smallest thing around, a tree, a leaf, a particle of dust.

It is that focus that becomes a meditation and that will center you, reveal the truth in all other things, and return you to your inner peace.

Chapter 4: April
APRIL 18

Holy spirit.

The gift of the spirit is not exclusive and not even a gift, it is more like an uncovering of what was always there, a revealing?

We all have the spirit within us, part of our DNA...Jesus revealed that to His disciples and in doing so, revealed it to us. To walk in His way, we need to intentionally access His grace and power, sometimes through faith, sometimes in knowing, sometimes by accident, but always.

Chapter 4: April
APRIL 19

Safety nets

Safety nets are constructed to enable a soft landing if you fall. That net embraces you and breaks both the fall, and the transition to solid ground. In that moment of falling, we have no sense of embrace, no sense that all will be good.

Then the safety net catches us, embraces us and brings us to safety. We tend to relax as the net allows us to transition oh so softly and safely to the ground and we begin again. This is how God protects us. Our nets are often not visible, but as we open ourselves to the knowledge they are there, they come rushing to cushion our fall more noticeably. They come in the form of a surprise meeting, words released from a book we opened, a sudden and direct ray of sunlight, a smile, a butterfly or flower or phone call.

Expect the safety net, relax a bit more during the fall, feel the embrace and begin again!

Chapter 4: April
APRIL 20

Your first flight

There is something strikingly different about knowing intellectually and knowing for sure. One comes from our mind, the other from our soul!

On my first flight, I remember marveling as the plane came through the clouds that covered the sky and entered full sunlight. There was a magic to that moment even though I intellectually knew the sun was hidden above the clouds, when I came through and saw it, I was in awe and wonder. There is a deeper understanding once you know for sure...kind of like a peace that passes all understanding!

I liken that moment to my embrace of God when the time comes in transition. I know intellectually there must be a supreme spirit hidden behind the clouds, but when I actually come through the clouds to the other side, I will know for sure and that will be Magic!

Chapter 4: April
APRIL 21

Purposed to 'be'

Do birds know they can fly or do they just fly? Does water know it flows or does it just flow? We human beings know and think too much, and in a strange twist of evolution, that advanced capability keeps us from doing what we are purposed to do!

In the end we need to evolve to a place where we can 'be'. We have to get out of our heads, tame the incessant stream of thoughts and "know" by being in the wonder, not in our heads. We need to live more into the truths of our 'being'.

Chapter 4: April
APRIL 22

What's next?

Ever wonder how we stumble into things? I believe we live in the possibility of a parallel world that exists along side us!

Every moment we engage in creates a sacred next moment, so if we are 'in' the now, our next moment will be different than it would have been if we were not as engaged! Think about this! What's next will more likely be different depending on how we engage the now!

In the movie sliding doors, we follow two paths of one person, one crafted as she just made a train for work and one as she misses that same train. These are seemingly meaningless differences.

Yet, we see a wholly different path...her two lives crisscross constantly, yet there is no moment truly the same but there is a parallel sameness that shows the persistent intention of God's plan that keeps bringing us opportunities to realign with Gods plan!

To some extent what is next depends on us. It can be more sacred if we engage, but at every instance that comes we need to decide again and again how to engage and inform the next holy moment. What's next in your life?

Chapter 4: April
APRIL 23

This too shall pass

When in the throws of pain or disappointment, if you wait long enough it passes. This is more often the case because all things are transient.

Some feel that God is always underneath there waiting for us to acknowledge Him in the pain.

When we can get to that holy space in the midst of pain or disappointment, we understand the meaning of 'this too shall pass' from a faith perspective too and that adds comfort to us all.

As reliably as the earth spins, all things pass and in the letting go of our attachments, all suffering ends. When we can let it go, it really goes.

Chapter 4: April
APRIL 24

Does it take two to dance!

That old saying, it takes two to dance has greater meaning than we usually place on it. There is a divine place in every dance and every interaction.

In these, God initiates the potential for great things. Think of an interaction between two people like this; envision God actually introducing us to this person we were about to engage, how different the interaction would be.

Consider this happening. "Bob this is Katie you will meet at the dessert table, she loves chocolate, is a single mom, and needs a job in marketing. Katie, this is Bob, he lives for chocolate, is a marketing consultant, and is a big brother in town." Imagine the possibilities in engaging now! Both of you will be more in tune with the others needs and how your gifts can be a support for each other's journey.

In real life, every interaction includes the power to engage at a deeper level like that. If we could take the time to not only see that extraordinary possibility but engage more intently this could become our way.

We would become more intuitive, more curious about the potential of this interaction and how we can serve. Imagine your world opened by this excitement!

The dance takes two, but it needs an overseer!

Chapter 4: April
APRIL 25

I'm fixing a hole

One of the most peaceful places for me is the beach. Water calms me, and sitting there amongst the incessant flow of waves slows my mind. I particularly like to see how the water rushes to shore and fills every hole, no matter how deep, then rushes back out. Water sometimes stays in the deeper holes awhile until it has softened it's edges and reduced its depth!

Love is like that, it rushes in and fills every hole, every pain - there is never a question of whether to fill one hole versus another, it's just filled.

In our life's choices we often allocate love as if it were a limited resource we need to protect. We pre-judge where our love should go like it was a finite commodity. Many times we choose which holes in our life to fill.

Love is not finite it is abundant. In freeing ourselves to love all things without prejudice, we open ourselves to love more and love all things. A holy love flows to all things; it fills them up regardless of how many holes are out there and how deep those holes are just like the ocean!

Holy love softens the depth and brings a oneness and a peace to the landscape we call life. All you need is love!

Chapter 4: April
APRIL 26

Like versus is

I often marvel at coincidences that occur and how when you are more aware or expectant of coincidence, it comes more often. Coincidence is an exposure of the spirit world that is often overwhelmed by the noise and pace of our modern lifestyle.

I like to connect more to that world and the universe around us and when we do, the metaphors "like" – blend into "is".

The opening of a flower is not like Gods design, it IS Gods design. Memories of a deceased loved one are not just like a comforting thought, it "is" a sacred visit! Thoughts of a dear friend in need are not like being with them, you are one with them.

The "like" blend into truth...the more we seek, the more we find!

Chapter 4: April
APRIL 27

Salmon rushing against the flow

I saw the movie, Salmon fishing in the Yemen. A story of faith both in finding a way to bring salmon to this barren place and in expecting the farm bred salmon to do what wild salmon do. The sub story to me is about our genetic code and whether our true selves can come forth after many generations of mutation or evolution that hide our true selves.

The salmon were farm bred...for generations they did not run against the current to return to their genetic space of spawning! Yet, somehow when released into the river they knew something was different, they had a calling, they would run.

In a strange way, I believe we humans are being called back to our true selves. We have been farm bred for generations by our ego and yet we are hearing a call from our inner spirit. We are Gods great partner in creation, the spirit is alive in all of us and calling. The call is getting louder in some and slowly, yet together, we turn and start to go upstream, just like the salmon.

Chapter 4: April
APRIL 28

The scientific process and failure

Engineers learn the discipline of scientific testing of hypotheses. Think, imagine, test, learn, and repeat! The underlying emphasis for success is seeing there is no failure, just ongoing learning on the way to discovery!

Discovery is something that takes discipline, perseverance, and faith.

Often we miss this in our daily life trials. We look upon mistakes, missed deadlines, love lost, expressed disappointments as failures. We sit with them too long as burdens rather than expectations in the discovery process we call life.

We need to see all failures for what they are, a label we wrongly apply and just the next step on our way to knowing! This change of perspective creates a world of benefit for our fragile ego's, and a life that could be changed forever.

Chapter 4: April
APRIL 29

Hunger games

I have both read the book and saw the movie 'the hunger games'. The storyline is of a young girl who steps forward to volunteer for these games of 'battle to the death' so that her younger sister is spared. That is a powerful insight into love!

At seminal points in our life, talk is cheap. Words don't work and we have to walk the talk and demonstrate truth as this heroine does! It is in these moments that our souls presence is the only communication that gets through!

Chapter 4: April
APRIL 30

Money is important isn't it?

This from a six year old who is hearing too often 'that is too expensive' or 'we need to wait for that fort'. I explained, 'Money is actually not Important at all, it is something that can be good or bad though.'

I made this comparison. Real important things like "love" and an "idea"' when they are shared they magically create more love and better ideas. This is how you know Importance because Gods hand creates more abundance for all!

Money can become this as well! When combined with Gods hand money can create more, like helping others, creating beauty, finding safety and peace for yourself and others, this is good and important things. Money can also be bad, so to be important it must be accompanied by good intention.

MAY 1

We cause our own suffering!

Buddha identified that attachment drives our pain. It is a difficult path to be human and not attach.

From the time we start being aware of ourselves, we attach to things that we call our own. From the two year old – saying "mine" to adults piling up material fortunes to which we identify. Over time, these things become important, they define us in a way.

Why would we define ourselves by things? Or titles? Or wealth? Try something out, unclutter just a little – see if you feel lighter OR anxious.

MAY 2

Cleansing our falls and failings

The forest is a sanctified place. As trees die and fall, they serve as the fertilizer for greater growth. Observing this natural order though is somewhat discomforting, out of order, chaotic.

But this is life's best lesson. The death of our dreams often fertilize new growth and greater dreams. Our grief in losing always precedes our joy of gaining. So, when we bury any of our sorrows, review our falls or recognize our failings, we need to do so without cleansing them and let it be as it is.

Fore in its natural state, it best serves to renew us and resurrect us!

MAY 3

Fall we must

It is early morning and I am reflecting on a bible passage. I sit in prayer reflecting on the night before Jesus' death. With all the turmoil around them, why couldn't his disciples stay awake?

This never made sense to me? Have you thought about this in any questioning way?

Knowing what comes next became a clue. The disciples were going to need historic strength to continue the ministry after Jesus' death. Where would that strength come from? Remember Peter, failing Jesus 3 times before realizing he had to harden himself to move forward. We all need a death of our own to renew.

So, the disciples took their own failures and fear and died to themselves. Jesus was a real God to them and His appearance in any form became their own resurrection.

The rest is history.

Chapter 5: May
MAY 4

Are you full or filling?

The mad hatter was a character much like me when I am over scheduled. I have back-to-back meetings today, a lunch date, and a board meeting tonight. So what do I do?

I scurry mindlessly chasing a schedule of my own making! No time to stop, no time to chat!

Is this a filling day or just a full day?

A full day leaves no space for filling! Moments will pass unnoticed. God's joys will pass too without wonder. To what end do we fill our days rather than find ways to make them filling?

Tomorrow, I will be a slave to the schedule I keep -- will it be full or filling?

Chapter 5: May
MAY 5

The current of our lives

The Genesee river roars through our city to become part of Lake Ontario. Its speed causes the water to assume a brownish color, a result of the strong currents churning the sands and silt as it flows through our city!

The river than settles into the Great Lake and to our view slows and clears.

In stillness, the water becomes so clear, its true spirit.

The current of our lives can churn us into a cloudy river like the Genesee, not allowing us to be still and reflect our true spirit. We need to seek time to settle and be still - in doing so, our muddied waters will clear and we will reflect our true selves more clearly to the world!

Chapter 5: May
MAY 6

Finding what fits!

Our grandson has show and tell every Monday. If he is visiting our property on Sundays, a walk in the woods usually finds something of interest. One day a complete birds nest offered up much discussion. How perfect and strong!

The close up viewing showed each twig to be whole, no pecking or scratching or cutting, they were made to fit the nest perfectly. This encouraged us to do some research and we found that birds often find the right fit for each twig. They don't try to force fit any material,

Much like a mason chooses rocks to build a stone wall. The smallest of creatures knows to let go of what doesn't fit, and better still, goes back out to find one that does.

All too often we struggle trying to make our circumstances or situations fit, when it may be best for us to give that up and find something else that fits. The building of our nest waits.

Chapter 5: May
MAY 7

Seeing through our own eyes

Imagine if our eyes were not connected to our brain and therefore had no reasoning attached to it? Everything we would see would have no name, and would attach no story!

Each viewing would be of a beautiful piece of art, extraordinary and expansive. Each viewing would hold a wonder that we could not ponder but somehow appreciate.

There are times my spirit allows me to be in that space often in the stillness of mid evening, a clear sky and bright moon and stars. I often stop and need to gaze in a peace that embraces me. Seeing from the spirit is in a way filtering out our thoughts and stories and letting that moment be as it is, unnamed, no story, extraordinary, one!

Chapter 5: May
MAY 8

Justice or just is?

Just what should we expect from justice? Life in its natural form is not just, it just is? Birds are sometimes hurt by a gust of wind; a fallen branch or a human step crushes ants. Is that injustice or is it just is?

When we accept what just is, we move toward a better place, our thoughts do not consume themselves in the unfairness that the mind creates. We can spend time holding each other up without judging.

It is there we will find the merger of just is and justice!

Chapter 5: May
MAY 9

Seeing differences

Often we fear differences! I see it or imagine it most in people. We see someone different and fear or judgment rings all the alarms.

We fall into a trap believing that one creation is better than another. We find ourselves for and against, liking and not liking.

At some point, we must see beyond the fear and judgment and see God in all things. In that way we will see our self in all things. When that happens, we can't see the differences fore the likes are too strong. We can't see the fear because love overcomes, and we cannot dislike when we see only ourselves!

Chapter 5: May
MAY 10

The eye of the storm

When satellites first showed us pictures of a hurricane from space, many marveled at the affirmation of the eye in the middle. Amongst the raw power and expanse of the storm, there stood at its center, peace and calm.

Wisdom recognizes this peaceful center for us to follow. In every storm there is a calm we can seek at our center. It will carry us through the worst storms and out to the sunshine that always follows!

Chapter 5: May
MAY 11

Being and doing

There is magic to being, and a completion in doing. Our God designed us uniquely to experience the blended capability of both being and doing!

Jesus sought time for 'being' and his 'doing' ministry of healing and justice was quite remarkable! As He lay the groundwork for his ministry to continue, He told his disciples to go out into the world and do what He did, clearly connecting 'being' and 'doing' as the formula to align the God within and bring that majesty to the world without.

Chapter 5: May
May 12

Cover-ups

We spend a lot of time trying to be something or someone else. Like actors who need to get into character, we put a new face on and assume another role every day that covers up who we really are. Remember the Beatles song, Eleanor Rigby who left her face in a jar by the door for no one – "all the lonely people"!

Why do we do this? We are hiding ourselves for fear of being known in our frailties and being vulnerable, and the one thing we do find is loneliness, the Beatles got that right.

Let your true face be seen, expose your wants and needs and become vulnerable. Drop the cover. You will be surprised at the freedom that awaits.

Chapter 5: May
May13

I feel fine

An early Beatle song is well known for the one guitar note that is struck and allowed to play out before any other note begins. I still enjoy that singular note, finding myself leaning into it as it plays itself out! You just want more music to happen but the note keeps playing and then it is no more.

It is a prophetic song structure in a way. The note represents our life and its suffering. Often we want that suffering to end (more notes to play) but what works best is to lean into that one solitary note until it is no more.

It is in that process of leaning into our pain and suffering that healing comes and we often begin to feel again.

The song then continues...'she's in love with me and I feel fine'.

Chapter 5: May
May 14

I win you lose.

We have gone to the extremes in society where we have to all win because we worry about people's feelings. Political correctness it is often called.

In athletic competition in particular we try to teach everyone wins rather than the more talented, prepared and practiced win. I wonder whether we are creating an injustice.

We need to teach 'how' everyone wins, rather than letting everyone win. Let me expound on that a minute.

There are ways of winning from a spiritual standpoint that creates an infinite abundance even in competition. For example, Both ideas, and love are expressions of unlimited winning. If I have an idea and I share it with you - we both now have the idea and it is possible that in the sharing, the idea becomes bigger making it possible we both have more then when we started. Love is similar in that sharing true love can create that feeling of giving yet receiving more in return. There is a miraculous Abundance inherent in those actions that we can share in all we do.

Let's bring this concept back to competition. If we teach the prepared, the skilled, the kind, the supportive, the role players and the stars all win, there is good we bring out of every loss as well as every win, and our children can identify their role in that competition. If we label it so - it is, and our kids will be better for it.

Chapter 5: May
May 15

The confronting of fear

Tony Robbins demonstrated his fire walk the other day on Oprah. People at his seminars are put into a place emotionally that they confront their fear of being burned with their minds first, and then proceed to do something here-to-fore unheard of! Like walk on hot coals!

We often are incapacitated by our fears...they keep us from stepping out and until the fear or pain is too much, we can't act. Robbins shows us that fear can be overcome now, don't wait for it to become crushing. Step out and free yourself with your mind.

Your thoughts will set you free!

Chapter 5: May
May16

Kissing the ground

The Pope often kisses the ground when he arrives in a new place as his first physical act. I often felt it was a blessing to God for a safe journey. I can see that action now as a humbling action, connecting the Pope as a humble servant of the people he will meet and serve in this new place.

Humbling oneself is the path to egoless servant hood. In "demonstrably" humbling our selves, a connection is opened to our true inner selves, our denying of our ego for the will to serve others. We need to create some demonstrable trigger in our lives to remind us to be humble servants in this world.

Chapter 5: May
May 17

Let go to see

Most boys have chased butterflies. The chase is half the fun, but a funny thing happens when you catch a butterfly, you fear hurting it!

So, if you are fortunate to catch one, you spread your hands ever so wide to give it room.

Then, you feel a desire to see its beauty, all the colors that make up its sensitive and fragile wings. But to see, you must let go. Letting go is the only way to reveal beauty and to see the truth...and so it is!

Chapter 5: May
May 18

Great friends

My wife has been blessed with great friends, so great there is room for me in the love that exudes from them. Friends are doorways to the things within us that God made so beautifully. Only friends have a way of seeing and embracing the good that we forget to look for in ourselves and forget we have in abundance.

Friends are the reminders that God loves me.

Chapter 5: May
May 19

Attracting Friends

Our friend Amy sent a time lapsed video of flowers blooming. Oh the miracle to see a flower bloom from the tight bud straining to be free to the burst of color, fragrance and nectar when it blooms.

It struck me in viewing the video that you can see bees' passing the bud over and over but when the flower blooms, the bee is right there. Similarly, if we can make it through the strains of life and get through the times where we are bound tight, we will bloom just where we are! Our unique color and fragrance and nectar will be visible to all, and we will attract all types of friends who wish to stay to pollinate our friendship.

If we stay tight, constrained and stressed in an unopen bud, we leave no room and we offer no attraction for others to come! In our blooming, we attract abundance.

Chapter 5: May
May 20

Banana grams

We recently learned this tile game. I love the way you build your own crossword and as the game proceeds you need to remake your words to make space for more tiles to be able to win. Sometimes you have to break down whole sections and start over to make enough room for more.

Life offers us many opportunities to change and grow and sometimes as in banana grams, we have to breakdown, and create space for more abundance. Abundance always waits in the spaces that we need to create.

Chapter 5: May
May 21

Worms

I remember as a boy seeing a worm cut and survive as two worms. Each part renews and grows to form a new life. Worms are valued parts of the life cycle, they eat and excrete to replace nutrients in the soil and their squirming around aerates the soil so that flowers and food grow more plentiful. They are renewal at its simplest.

Perhaps when we feel cut into two or broken, we can use the worm as our example; Be humble, seek simplicity, and do the work of aerating our own soil to heal, renew, and prepare for new growth!

Chapter 5: May
May 22

You could be right

I saw this lady being interviewed last week and expressing that when she is confronted or criticized by friend or foe she can honestly answer 'you could be right' and move on! This is a great example of an ego in check. Among all the possible histrionics and suffering caused by being criticized, if we are true to our inner self, those comments are all labels that have no lasting truth and in fact when we can say 'you could be right' rather than believing them, we give them a half life in being able to hurt us.

Their power is gone twice as fast and we move on!

Chapter 5: May
May 23

No thing

Buddha's name when strictly translated means 'no thing'. This is a striking admonition of our egoic thoughts of self-importance, power and glory.

We are truly 'no thing'!

I often reflect on the message of humbling ourselves to nothing as the goal and purpose of our time on earth. When we are 'in being' as a 'no thing' we create a heightened alertness, of being awake and more aware of all other things. We see connectedness around us when we no longer see ourselves above it all.

Remarkably, 'no thing' becomes 'one with all things!'

Chapter 5: May
May 24

Pain bodies

Eckhart Tolle identifies barriers human beings have from evolving toward enlightenment. One of the most powerful of these barriers is something he calls Pain bodies. They are old wounds that come back unannounced and cause over reaction to a situation or event in the present time.

Sometimes pain bodies are so strong they are even genetically placed on our DNA! We all have them at some level. To grow through the pain body we need to become aware of its existence because when we can 'see' the pain body, we are in fact beginning to separate from it. Our soul becomes engaged to bring light to the darkness.

It is here we begin to understand the old pains can no longer hurt us and that we are hurting ourselves by giving these memories power. They lose their hold ever so slightly and in time the light of the soul replaces them.

Chapter 5: May
May 25

The ring of fire

Every year friends of ours celebrate an old Native American tradition called the ring of fire. All residents of the lake buy flares or create fires on the water line. What a sight of natural beauty and personal reflection. It's message burns on my soul.

We all have fires in our lives; some are flares neat and contained, some roaring fires that could be out of control in short order. We stand facing our fires!

During our life events, we often fear going through the flame to salvation, and we wait for our fires to go out instead and this rarely works. Jumping through or facing the flame is what faith is about.

We do risk more pain, yet when we can stand up to or jump through our fears, we can find the embrace of our God beyond and a new day.

Chapter 5: May
May 26

Using sadness

We often are sad. I don't know exactly the number of times sadness falls upon me, but it is quite a number. I am capable at times of diverting my sad feelings with positive thoughts and if the sadness was created by my own minds projections, I have learned to overcome them.

There are however times of deeper sadness that hit our souls directly. These cannot be as easily dealt with and we often need to go through the sadness to heal. It is this deeper sadness like losing a loved one, a pet, yourself, that may need another approach to transform the sadness into something good.

Here we need to engage the soul in something transformative. There is ageless wonder in the art of "creating" that transforms us, whether that be painting a canvass, turning a potters wheel, or writing a poem.

Our sadness becomes part of the creation process and its energy is released into that tangible expression of your creation! Whatever the creative expression that emerges, you can leave it there, and move on.

Chapter 5: May
May 27

Think twice, act once?

The old carpenters wisdom of measure twice and cut once is a pointer toward wisdom.

In terms of managing our thoughts though we are presented with a paradox. No amount of thinking can fix a problem brought by the same thinking!

Einstein identified that in solving problems that we ourselves create by our thinking, biases and limitations, we need to seek a new outlook to solve the problem.

We are thought filled creatures, and in all this mind chatter, we normally think our way to a solution that our thinking has created. It is that thinking that causes problems to remain.

We need to stop the thoughts and constant chatter and center ourselves to a new place to bring a new solution. It is then that a new outlook will come to bring a solution that is real. Then we are free to act with confidence.

Chapter 5: May
May 28

Oneness

The Sufi prophet Ghalib writes the raindrop is most joyous in entering the river. We (our souls) are similarly joyful when we experience our oneness with the universe.

It is then we feel a belonging and a true peace that there is a vast mystery we don't fully understand, but we are part of it!

Chapter 5: May
May 29

Using a fire to burn

When given the choice of escaping a deadly fire, what is it we will bring with us? What if you had time to prepare for your fire?

Imagine being told there will be a major fire coming next month, get ready! With time, we would most likely save more because all things have or can be believed to have attachment and therefore lasting value.

Life at its center is reflected in the crisis of deciding just what do you really need. A life lived well can be about paring down to only those life necessities left to cherish. We misunderstand the necessity of taking the clutter from our lives, and leaving the true value of what is left as life.

We all need to make choices in preparation of our own fires!

Chapter 5: May
May 30

The mystery of moments

How do we live more in the moment? This is the big question the mystics have put forth for all of us. I often see our lives as being lived in two worlds that co-exist, spirit time and earthly time.

Spirit time is where each moment is forever because time as we know it does not exist. Earthly time is where we are influenced by every day life around us; our thoughts, ego and responsibilities.

Earthly time overwhelms both spirit time and us in general.   But imagine they co-exist and you have choice to go back and forth.

If you were to ask most people, they would say life is a string of distinct, seemingly disconnected moments! Life happens.

When we are immersed in spirit time, somehow that 'overwhelming' thought disappears and we transcend time, as we know it. We are just "in time" and we sometimes get lost in that time. You will spirit time most when you are caring and serving others and in the process of creating.

That is the point of mystery for me. How do we discover how to be more in spirit time? We do have choices to step away from the pace and become one with the spirit at varied moments during the day.

If there is a secret to living in spirit time more consistently, it seems to lie in that moment "we" decide to reside for a while in what is "happening" or move on.

Chapter 5: May
May 31

Passive resistance

What is it about passive resistance that creates great people and globally significant change? Think about Buddha, Jesus, Ghandi, Mandela, and Martin Luther King, and what they have brought upon this earth. Their resistance without violence brought great change because it was not about them but a higher ideal.

There is nothing more powerful than aligning your soul with the Holy Spirit and acting upon it. Justice prevails in these circumstances because it is right.

Chapter 6: June
June 1

Me and my shadow

Our shadow is always there copying our every move.

In the middle of all circumstances, whether they bring joy or suffering, not far behind is always a change of sorts and that change often depends on how we look at things. It seems to be an unmistakable truth to me that the good and bad are always close behind.

Having said that, our perspective helps define what we make out of each circumstance; if we bring light to every encounter whether that is good or bad – like walking toward the Sun, our shadow is always behind us, if we however approach an encounter with fear or hesitation we in effect turn our back on the light and our shadow walks before us!

It's you and your shadow doing this dance we call life, it's your choice whether to lead or follow.

Chapter 6: June
June 2

Touching

We have two cats, sisters Lola and Grace. We took them home from their adoption center when they were quite young. They would sleep hugging each other as that touch brought them peace as they adjusted to life with us. There is something about having no pretense and just trusting what felt real and peaceful.

I find myself touching a lot. I often wake from a sleep and desire a connection with my wife at that smallest level, if only a toe or a finger, the connection always seems divine and brings me a peace.

Michelangelo's fresco in the Vatican depicts our God reaching a finger out to us, just needing that slight touch! There is a peace and trust in touch that even God desires. Touch creates a place where two beings transform into one.

Chapter 6: June
June 3

Hurting ourselves

Why do we revisit and linger on our personal hurts so that they hurt us again and again?

This phenomenon is common to most people. It reflects our humanness and sensitivities, our shortcomings and vulnerable places. We actually build our ego to provide us protection from all these perceived shortcomings. We hope that will protect us from being exposed and feeling pain, but in doing so they hide the true us.

Our true self, our 'being' is already whole and worthy. Our being would tend to let go of any pain, seek forgiveness, and diminish any lasting impact on our soul.

Our being recognizes that in this current moment we are not being hurt again, it is our own thoughts of past pain and future fears that make pain real to us now.

So let go of that pain that comes back. It cannot hurt you now.

Chapter 6: June
June 4

Overcoming limitations

We have a friend Stuart who has one arm. He lost it in an accident when younger, and his spirit overcame that tragedy! He can do anything and do it well.

Our souls evolve despite limitations and many times because of our limitations! Being faced with a limit is the surest way to go beyond that limit when the spirit engages to do so.

Little chicks incubate in their eggs and grow and grow by eating the fluids around it. As they grow and eat the food within their contained space, they become fearful and they begin to peck at their limitations frantically (the walls of the egg) until they break through the walls. To their surprise, they fall out the other side of the egg wall and are born again, opening up the new world for them to explore.

In all limitations, our hearts need to crack open to overcome them and experience real joy. In every limit, there is a big beyond!

Chapter 6: June
June 5

Receiving gifts

How often do you hesitate taking a next step because it is not what you expected, nor dreamed? My friend Ray tells me this story. There was this farmer in ancient China who had a wonder horse. The horse was known to be the greatest working horse in the area, providing mightily for his farmer!

One day, during a storm the horse became frightened and ran away. Many mourned the loss and offered condolences! The farmer however did not react sadly and many were perplexed. Days passed and the farmer worked hard on his farm with no visible regrets. Then in a couple of days the horse returned with a half dozen wild friends bringing even greater abundance to the farmer. His friends were so joyful for him and wished to have a big party, yet the farmer did not react and again, they were perplexed. The farmers reaction is the blessing. In our daily lives, each step we take or choice we make is an opportunity to accept what is, rather than what we want it to be. Disappointment never comes in these circumstances!

When we accept every new moment as a gift waiting for us, the gift of the unknown, we will be happiest.

Chapter 6: June
June 6

Space and time

I watched a film on the Hubble telescope. Seeing live pictures of the beginning formations of galaxies billions of years ago. The universe is so large that it has taken millions of years for its light to reach us so that we can see! So we are actually seeing "live" something that occurred long ago.

This enlightened me to the fact that time really is an illusion! How does our feeble mind grasp this concept of seeing live the deep past?

This helps me make sense of the glory of God in another way - in time and space? Einstein surmised that at the speed of light (or infinite speed) time stood still, and therefore since God lives in the spirit, that space or 'no time' is where God resides.

Then this possibility opens to me. When we are with God, time is still and for all eternity we are consoled in that one embrace. That moment is the one true moment that contains eternity.

I am more at peace knowing I don't know it all but I also know that God does.

Chapter 6: June
June 7

Projecting

We all project our own thinking or opinions onto others and in doing so believe they are true.

My mom kept me from dogs because of her fear of dogs! Her projecting of her fears onto me obviously made little sense and in fact prevented me from enjoying the gift of incessant love as a boy that caring for a dog provides. I saw this many years later as I was blessed with my first dog, and I thought how restricting projection could be on others.

We must be both aware of and own our projections, fore it is then that we can remove the limits we unknowingly create on others as well as ourselves.

Chapter 6: June
June 8

Rest in all things

Buddha talks about finding rest in the great tree from all storms and all praise. Today is my anniversary. During our wedding we read a Kahil Gibran story of the two great trees growing together yet apart. Buddha found the tree a place of rest and protection from the storms of life.

Trees are something to behold. In a storm, trees stand strong to brave the powers of nature and without hands to hold on, they can let go of the wind's fury. In the warmth and light of sunshine, the great tree stands tall with its leaf span to protect us from the heat.

The tree brings peace because it accepts what is, does not judge them and does not hold on to any of the fury. Perhaps like the great trees, we should stand strong to face the fury yet let it pass without holding on to it.

Perhaps we can grow stronger and taller together in the protection of each other. There, we too can find rest, peace and joy! The Kahil Gibran message of the tree was just right for a wedding reading.

Chapter 6: June
June 9

Signs of cracking

We visited the Washington monument after the latest earthquake. The once powerful structure seemingly built with solid stone showed signs of stress cracks everywhere. The rebuilding process includes extensive work on both the inside and the outside, and avoids the easy fix of just filling the cracks!

We too can buckle under the stress that comes through prolonged or sudden cracks in our life. When we do, God acts as the master mason - trying to bring our inner and outer lives together with extensive work. it is important to take the time to do this work and avoid the quick fixes we tend to seek. Sometimes we even need to tolerate the crack for awhile as the rebuilding work is done. God blesses the cracks, big or small and works us in and out until we are renewed for another day!

Chapter 6: June
June 10

The spaces

In the smallest atom there is more space than protons, neutrons and electrons, much more, in fact it is mostly space! Space exists in all things no matter how solid they appear. The universe as vast as our minds can imagine is more space than matter. A hard piece of wood or a tree is even more space than matter.

So what does this represent? Space on its own suggests an emptiness, nothing...'no thing'! This is spiritually noteworthy as space is actually where everything of value happens.

Space is a pointer to what is holy! Space, like the space between our thoughts or the space between our 'exhale and inhale' are places to revere. They are all holy.

Space is everywhere and plentiful but we need to find those empty spaces and stay there awhile. It is there in stillness we will find God.

Chapter 6: June
June 11

Share and have more?

Here is a paradox worth thinking about. Sharing something that increases what you have. When this occurs, God is present in a holy moment.

When you share most things, like a book or a toy - the act itself does not usually create more of that same thing. A Holy sharing somehow creates more, sort of like the fishes and the loaves miracle in the feeding of the 5,000 where Jesus shared two fish and a few loaves of bread with 5,000 people and had more left over than when He started.

With intention, we can share these holy moments everyday! For example, we can share an idea with the intention of helping another and it magically grows when another receives it and builds on it! The same is true of love, as when freely and intentionally given, multiplies the love back to you! I see sharing with intention as a pointer toward God and something we should do to our hearts content.

Chapter 6: June
June 12

Mutant changes

There are periods of time in human evolution that we made giant leaps as a people! I was visiting the museum of natural history and viewing their human evolution exhibit. There is this great display showing the size of the human brain over millions of years and the display made it clear how slow changes occurred until all of a sudden (in relative terms) there we were! Scientists attribute the capability to build tools and therefore hunt meat (protein) as the most likely cause for that brain growth.

In a spiritual sense, this also was the beginning of a new relationship with God. We became evolved enough to create an ego to make sense of what we were becoming and what we observed.

Both the separation from God reflected in the Adam and Eve story, and the beginning of understanding of a God's existence grew in us. Gods plan is unfolding in evolution and if we could see our souls in that same museum exhibit it would be just as clear of a giant leap!

Chapter 6: June
June 13

The miracle of 'more than One'

I have heard many lessons of the miracle on the mount, and feeding of the 5000. There are two stories that stand out for me. One, Jesus took the bread and broke it, blessed it and shared it. Bishop TD Jakes says the miracle is in the breaking! The openness that is created in the breaking creates the space for healing and miracles to occur.

The second, I believe from Marcus Borg, is a practical explanation and 'twist' of just what was the miracle.

Living was difficult at that time in history, and when a family would go on a pilgrimage or long trip as they were coming to the Temple, many by necessity carried food that was just enough for their family to survive the trip, and was not often shared due to personal survival concerns and needs. It was precious and guarded as so. After hearing The Sermon on the Mount, Jesus opened the hearts of many and as the baskets circulated, people actually put some of their hidden food in the basket for others to share. This is a storyline we see happening even today where an inner voice speaks to us, and we share, often acting in love for a stranger.

The 5,000 is a story of the "more than one", we need only to seek to share in love in this moment with one other, and God multiplies it for us, sometimes inexplicably to thousands.

Chapter 6: June
June 14

Feeling each other versus seeing

I was admiring my wife of nearly forty years with our grandson recently and I was reminded of why I love her so much. It was startling in a way, because there is a time in a close relationship that you stop looking at the beauty of the picture, but you become one with the picture! We have been in the same picture for many years enjoying being one and over time you forget you 'are' the picture. I came to thinking whether this was taking her for granted. There is no longer a seeing, but a knowing and a being. As humans, we can sometimes mistake that for a distance between us rather than an integration among us that suggests no distance. Through the miracle of love we are transformed into the glorious picture created for others to see and for us to feel.

Chapter 6: June
June 15

Can you live with the question?

I love jeopardy. Putting your answer in the form of a question is brilliant! We humans have troubles with questions. We need answers to avoid the anxiety of not knowing. But yet we know so little as it relates to Godly things.

The questions outnumber the answers and that creates discomfort in many. That paradox will stay with us until we know everything or we accept through faith that we just don't know.

If we live too much in the questions, we may actually miss the truth.

Chapter 6: June
June 16

Friends and lovers

The poetry of The Beatles always struck me as divine in many ways. 'of all our friends and lovers, some are gone, some remain....but in my life, I loved you more'!

I look at the tapestry of life and I see that there is often one friend or lover that is loved more. We tend to seek a deepness with very few and a unity with one. Yet, we have the capacity to love at the deepest level with all friends and lovers. Love is abundant and expansive, and surprisingly knows no limits.

Chapter 6: June
June 17

Watercolor

I love to see the aqua colors of the ocean in the Caribbean. Water on its own knows no color, but it reflects the glory of its natural environment.

As spiritual beings we need to be like water.   In many ways it is a pointer to the divine. Be clear, be ourselves, reflect the glorious colors inside us, embrace those who enter, guide those who float by, and when in turbulence stand still to find your innate clarity.

Chapter 6: June
June 18

Guests that overstay their welcome

We had a great aunt that came to stay with us when I was younger. She had a young boy and looking back it must have been hard for my family. I recall they over stayed their welcome, staying for months and left under some level of disharmony.

When we have a pain that stays with us, we need to invite it to leave. Letting it stay and go on interrupting our life is not a formula for happiness. Take some time to sit with your pain, understand its reason for being, recognize it need not hurt you any longer, and ask it to leave.

In that release, you gain your freedom. Help your pain pack up and wish it well. Your home is back!

Chapter 6: June

June 19

Magnifying our life

I remember being fascinated by taking a magnifying glass and focusing the light on a dry leaf and creating a fire! When we confine and focus ourselves so obsessively on certain parts of our life or problems, we can ignite a fire and create more problems.

When we step back and broaden our horizons, we open new worlds, create space for positive thought, and make room for healing to work. Through that simple act of expansion we will begin healing and find hope in the broader picture.

Chapter 6: June
June 20

Pain that stays

Our adopted daughter has MS. It is a terrible disease and she lives daily with pain and side affects that would sideline most people. I marvel at her desire to live normally and overcome such debilitation.

I often wonder how does she and others live with never ending pain? One clue I have found is that deep inside our souls we are already healed, there is no physical pain, nor mental anguish and we can separate ourselves from the physical body we are inhabiting. I believe that is where those who suffer greatly go to survive.

So is true for all of us. We have that place to go for comfort and a peace that passes understanding, we need to find ways to go there more and stay awhile.

Chapter 6: June
June 21

Light reflects us too

Light reveals itself by reflecting objects of His creation! We often see God in His revealed beauty such as a flower, the ocean or a beautiful, breathtaking vista. What we often miss is outside of our sight - us.

We too are revealed as God in the same way that all His other creations are revealed Once that revelation sinks in, how can we look at ourselves or any other magnificent human again without wonder and awe! Like the great vistas, we are

God revealed to others.   We need do nothing except be us!

I am humbled in our human understanding of that magnificence, and I believe that all other creations, the flowers and the mountains rejoice in seeing us! I shall never gaze at another's face in the same way.

Chapter 6: June
June 22

Clamming

Ever clam? The process is rigorous: The tide goes out, the clams that could not ride the tide are left on shore although buried in the sand. to find them, you dig!

Much like cycles of our life, if we don't ride the tide and resist, we can get buried in the sand behind. In those cases, it takes some digging to free us. Then when it seems you can't dig out, a new tide comes in and frees us from the sand, and we have another opportunity to ride the tide out or resist again.

Life's cycles come and go, if we ride the tide we are more apt to be free, if we resist we are more apt to be buried. Go with the tides!

Chapter 6: June
June 23

Success and fame

Being a celebrity and famous creates a counter point to true happiness and therefore creates happiness gaps we see so readily in our society. Just think about the largeness of the ego and how that separates us from our true self.

We are most fulfilled when we recognize all people as special not just a few and certainly not just ourselves! In pursuit of fame or celebrity we create a longing for more versus less, we tend to begin thinking that fame is filling, when only love is. As Mark Nepo says quite prophetically, we need to 'celebrate being' versus 'being a celebrity. '

Chapter 6: June
June 24

Dance our feelings

Our grandson is a growing, lanky six year old who has bundles of energy. He often will be walking and dancing concurrently, his arms and legs awkwardly flailing to some internal music. I believe inside of him is an expression of feelings and joy that manifest in his dance and it must be a form of joyful expression.

We adults hold those feelings in, digest them and sometimes deny them. I believe denial of joyful expression creates ailments of the body, mind and spirit. Through some kind of embodiment of those joyful feelings we can heal ourselves. Our grandson instinctively knows.

Chapter 6: June
June 25

"And In The end, the love you take is equal to the love you make" Lennon & McCartney

The equality of things in our universe is an expression of a creative intelligence! Physics keeps learning and finds that there is an eternal evenness and the deeper physics digs the more we affirm. For example, energy is not lost, it is moved, shared, exchanged, in fact infinitely created! Abundant! Love works the same way.

The law of Abundance is a unifying theory that energy works toward a purpose. When you give love, you get it back. When you withhold love it is withheld. So, in the end, you are what you reap. Reap well.

Chapter 6: June
June 26

Pray for gratitude

Ghandi tells us that to pray is not always asking. We often pray for things rather than praying in thanks for what we have already. There is a correlation that the grace we receive in our lives comes from being grateful for what we already have.

But there is another part of Ghandi's stream of thought, as he goes on to say that 'it is better in prayer to have a heart without words, than Words without heart'!

So in the ultimate discussion with God, Our intent means more, it is the way to connect with those invisible energy streams flowing into our soul, and out to our world. Every answered prayer starts with being heard and sometimes that means without words. If we pray in gratitude and in love we are full. If we pray in want and need we are empty regardless of how many words we use.

Chapter 6: June
June 27

A serious student

I remember being a serious student in that I did not have time for fun, or perhaps I made it that way. There was too much academic work, and a lot of real work for school payments.

I recall now a story of the Zen teacher telling his student to find enlightenment at the rivers edge. He would become a serious student of the water, listening to what the water had to teach him. He studied and contemplated for days. He was so serious and focused until he was interrupted by these young children running and playing in the river. They were so joyfully splashing about and so lost in their enjoyment they never recognized his serious needs.

He complained to his Zen master that he could not finish his work because of these children. His Zen master stared at him and after a long pause said quietly, "it was the children who heard what the water was telling them, while you were still listening!"

Our lives are full of difficult times and full of times we mark serious. Our active responses or serious contemplations make it difficult to listen for the messages that are there all the while we worry or study.

Listening deeply is a passive response where we give all judgment away, and listen through a filter of compassion. If we can do that, we will have transformed the difficult time into a lesson learned. We will have become a serious student!

Chapter 6: June
June 28

Driving

I drove 12 hours today for a two hour meeting. It was a wonderful ride on a beautiful day. I thought about being in control as the driver. I reflected on how my wife is the classic back seat driver. She wants to control all things without the controls. Who drives, how fast they drive, how they pass, how they navigate or their lack thereof! Why do we care so much as the passenger? What difference does it really make?

We control our lives the same way we do as back seat drivers. God controls the ride, yet we want to. Who is really driving in our life's story? All evidence would tell us it is not us. Taking control when we are not in control creates much mayhem and in the large life story, the same thing happens as in the car! The back seat driver really makes the ride miserable, questioning nearly everything, the speed, the choice of route, the internal comfort, the driving of others around us! They miss the beauty of the ride. The views are bountiful, the interactions richer and in the end the journey is better.

Sit back, relax and enjoy the ride.

Chapter 6: June
June 29

Moving evolution!

Evolution is not just survival of the fittest, science has found a mutant genetic component as well which along the way allows any species to leap forward.

These two parts of evolving work together and form what sticks! Where does this 'mutant leap' come from and can we influence something that looks random?

Being the human species, we can uniquely think about our own need for genetic change, so I suggest that we can participate in that creation story and influence evolution more than we think.

It is becoming more commonly agreed in spiritual circles that we can co-create the future world by being intentional in the moment. Could we then deduce that it is possible to co-create our own evolution? Hmmm

Chapter 6: June
June 30

Errors of omission

I have always felt strongly that to deny the truth was as strong a sin as ignoring the situation that confronts you. Omission seems to me is a tool of the ego to make us feel better about looking away!

This does no ultimate good. Our inner self knows and if we can, our ability to avoid omission will define us more at the end of the day and our true self emerges.

Heart matters

Recent scientific experiments are proving that the heart really does carry emotion. In the quiet time between gathering in blood and sending out blood there is a space. The heart uses this space to calibrate our inner feelings and emotions and then adjusts the blood makeup to reflect what it measures. So, if we have inner peace the blood makeup carries stimulants or elevators to the brain, reinforcing the positive mood. If the heart senses danger, or fear it would carry chemicals to assure alertness and tension.

This explains so much to me particularly the concept of " you are what you think". Since the body cannot differentiate real versus imaginary thoughts, if we are thinking positive, the heart reinforces that feeling and we actually become happier.

Mental disease

I saw the movie 'I am' last night. It is a story of a highly successful movie director who had a near death biking accident and as a result of a long recovery period, he wanted to explore why the world seemed crazy.

He started interviewing many people from all walks of life looking for a mental disease that caused our world to be as it is. He found a dis-ease but it was centered more in western societies desire for wealth and things and how that has become our "right view".

The author found that as a result of chasing these western values, we potentially distort or worse, miss the essence of life. In ancient languages such as Hindu, the word for mental health was 'wrong view'! Our primal human values called for cooperation and sharing for the tribe to survive, which in ancient language was interpreted as the 'right view'! Ancient peoples knew that if you were selfish or greedy it hurt the whole tribe and this behavior was a dis-ease of significance to all!

As humans evolved and became smarter about things like farming and using tools to hunt we began to specialize and isolate versus cooperate and share. Just a few people's efforts could then feed the community versus their shared roles, progress as it was thought. However, this combination of events enabled the wrong view to seep into our consciousness in many ways without an appropriate right view replacement or challenge.

In a funny way, we need to get back to what we knew before we were so learned!

Chapter 7: July
July 3

Quantum entanglement

This term was created by Einstein. In particle experiments, he recorded odd behaviors of particles and although he could see it and repeat it, he could not explain it. It seemed that after electrons were used in an experiment circling each other for example, they were allowed to spin off in opposite directions. However, Einstein noted that as scientists subsequently manipulated one of the electrons in another experiment, it's former partner in the testing immediately reacted the same way as the partner as if they were being manipulated together! How was this possible?

Quantum entanglement proves the mysterious connections of all things. We are part of a universe that Interacts constantly to keep everything in balance and connected!

When I think about that more intently, I marvel even more so at being in the moment and our real impact on the world around us! This very moment is part of what the next moment brings and so if we are embracing the moment with intention, we become part of creation. Our intent impacts our moment, which impacts others. If we are joyous and coming from love, we are creating a better tomorrow.

With that small act, I am being the change I want to see in the world, as Ghandi expressed so well.

Chapter 7: July
July 4

Democracy in nature

A funny thing happens with the onset of any new learning or new technology. We seem to peel away another layer of understanding creation. In the use of advanced digital photo technology we are able to study nature up close and personal. While studying formations - like a herd of deer, it was found that the herd somehow communicated as one to change direction or run. Slow motion photography allowed us to see that in split seconds, the deer would one-by-one show an alertness to a threat for example by raising their head...as more and more did so, there was this inherent counting and voting occurring. When the alertness reached 51% they took off as one. This happens over and over in many animal formations including birds, and science has concluded it was not randomly occurring, but a miracle of nature. We by our existence in nature are meant to cooperate and share, to work closely together, to be democratic!

As fits all theories of evolution, this natural instinct gives us a better chance of surviving and thriving. Being July 4th independence day, leads us to consider the divine providence in our constitution and declaration. Our founders knew the basic connection of our spirits and our inalienable right granted by our creator to be free, and to pursue life, liberty and happiness. Democracy ends up being a divine plan for our very survival!

Chapter 7: July
July 5

Heart matters - tuning in!

The heart emits an electronic field that can be measured outside our bodies. Jill Bolte Taylor wrote in her book 'the stroke of insight' that when she lost her entire left side of the brain in a stroke, she could sense immediately the energy of all people! When someone entered her room, she knew that they were kind or not, that they cared or not and whether they were safe or not without a word being shared.

How often do you get a feeling that everything is ok or not when you enter a room? That is an example of the energy that exists all the time around us. We are genetically programmed to communicate at that higher level of energy and while we grow into our promise, we have to create the still spaces in our mind to connect more deeply. Just like radio waves running past us, if we are not tuned to the right frequency we can't hear the songs!

Tune in, there is so much playing around us.

Chapter 7: July
July 6

Problem solving

I am a trained engineer and problem solving was a finely tuned skill learned, and honed by experience. I so often move into problem solving mode, that I miss the intangible elements of life surrounding the problem. I am learning gratefully!

How often do you jump into solving the problem for yourself or others? Our human interactions frequently include a statement such as 'I am not feeling well or I am lonely, or I worry! We immediately shift into behaviors to resolve the feeling when quite often the solution is to just sit with the feeling. Don't do anything except 'be'!

How soothing that premise is - to understand that action is not always the solution . how much easier it is to just 'be', and how clear the so called problem will be in its aftermath.

Chapter 7: July
July 7

Waiting

Lao Tzu talks about patience as one of the foundations of living, letting life come to us.

Fear or pain comes with a need to act, to rid us of the discomfort. When we can find the patience and strength to wait before acting, we allow time to flow over the issue, like water flowing over a deep hole and filling it!

Time brings access to truth and allows us the gift of a deeper perspective that all things pass and we need to take more time in all things.

When you feel it necessary to act quickly find a way to stall, go inside for a level of peace and discernment, let things unfold before you. The hole your pain created will be filled and smoothed and you will become more whole, less fearful as a result.

Chapter 7: July
July 8

The pattern of Moments

My wife and I were chatting at how connected our grandson is to moments versus things. When you think back in your life on special times, more likely a moment brings warmth and light, and our memories become streams of those moments!

Theologians talk about pointers, meaning that we can acquire no real knowledge of the ultimate truth, just pointers to truth! Moments are pointers!

Making cookies with grandma, morning time in bed, telling stories, holding a child to relieve a pain, working together on something grown up, helping someone with problems bigger than yours, forgiving are the moments of your life that point to the truth in our lives!!

Chapter 7: July
July 9

Ride the waves

The shoreline is the roughest, most unforgiving part of the ocean! Yet, we long to be in the water at the riskiest spot where waves come crashing in, and the undertow goes crashing out.

Great swimmers know to swim more in the deep outside these risk areas and surfers have learned to use the power of the wave floating above it.

Life can be like the shoreline. Each time we are faced with the unexpected turmoil's of life, we find ourselves in the wave that is crashing to the shore and in the turbulence we are flipped and turned and thrown back out in the strong undertow!

Imagine that you can sit above the wave or swim outside it in the deep? In this case, you don't fight the power of the wave, but use it to elevate your spirit above it all. By accepting the turmoil, you can avoid the crashing in and the undertow pulling you back out.

Life is much easier lifting you above the chaos and observing the turmoil as it passes.

Chapter 7: July
July 10

It is hard to hate up close

Governor Christie of New Jersey was quoted as saying this as it relates to bi-partisan efforts in governing. How true this is in all things!

Knowing eliminates a lot of fear and pain and overcomes ignorance. One of the surest cures for the fear of flying is to take lessons in aerodynamics, the fear of insects is to be with an expert who shows there is nothing to fear, etc.

The opposite of fear is love and knowing always brings us closer to love by diminishing fear! Discrimination and bias are behavioral fears of ignorance. If we take the time to know what we fear, that fear collapses. Find a way to get closer to that fear. Research it, talk to it, hug it, embrace it...it will melt away.

Reading ahead

My wife has an interesting habit of reading ahead. She will constantly read the ending of a chapter or a book and know how it is going to turn out while she is still reading the book. Would it be possible, would we do the same thing with our lives? Look ahead to see how an event or our life turned out and come back to the 'now' complete with that knowledge or wisdom? Would we do something different or does the knowing give us peace in the moment?

I believe there is a paradox at play when we consider our role in creating the future. When we are truly in the moment, we are in the only future that exists! Our actions in the now help form the next moment which is just like reading ahead.

So maybe my wife has it right. Live the 'now' with more knowing and passion because it is the future that we are creating!

Making waves in the bath

Watching a child play in a bathtub is magic. They twist in the water, and guide themselves through waves of their own creation. In life, we often create our own waves and then get carried away by them rather than twisting around them or working through them.

Children teach us to twist through the waves, enjoy them and embrace them! Then, like the children we can work through it rather than being carried away. After working through it, we can get out of the tub, clean and ready for anything!

Illusion and seeing what is real

I saw David Copperfield the illusionist a few times and it got me thinking about what is real because I was obviously easily fooled! Then I took the course in miracles, a program that is designed to unlearn all we have learned to more easily see the truth in all things. The underlying premise is that in fact, everything is an illusion. In the early exercises, we spend time un-naming things. For example, the tree is only a tree because we name it so, in reality, it just is.

The essence of the work is to understand all things are an illusion of our thoughts and mind and not real and distinct the way we have labeled them. All things are connected and just exist when seen free of our learned bias. The course in miracles teaches us that thoughts are the cause of all effects in our life and the way we label events is similar to labeling things, it is not real as we label it, it only is.

When we can see things without a Label and without attachment, we begin to see the truth, and the oneness of all things.

Chapter 7: July
July 14

Know thyself

My grandson is the son of Sudanese African parents, and he was telling me that he and three other classmates were putting on a class play about wild cats. The kids made it up, and were to present it the next day. He played the black cat.

I immediately tensed in hopes he was not stereotyped or discriminated against, but I caught myself and asked, are you the black cat because of your dark skin?

He quickly said 'no, I like black cats.' I saw in his answer the innocence and truth in knowing thyself.

There are roles we assign ourselves and those we live out and most of those trappings are not our true selves...'I like black cats' is a truth.

Chapter 7: July
July 15

Touching

My wife is in Florida moving her 91year old dad to a new home! As unfortunate luck would have it, he fell the morning of the move and was highly disoriented and weak. My wife was telling me how he was unable to walk, and he was not making any sense when he attempted to talk and then as if seeking a way to release his pain, he began speaking his native Italian.

Julie, a dear friend and like a second daughter began massaging his feet and legs as she prepared him for a nights rest, instinctively knowing touch was healing! It gave him comfort of a holy kind and he rested!

Touch is healing. Jesus most often used touch in healing others. Children seek touch - a kiss or a hug to soothe their pain.

Touch emits a positive energy that spreads through us, connecting us to each other and elevating our spirits. Much like spreading butter on warm bread, it seeps deep, enfolds the bread and the bread and butter become one. Touch is a life giving impulse reminding us that a full life needs to express fully in every sense and in every dimension, when we are saturated, we are one, we heal!

Chapter 7: July
July 16

Divine memory

I am in awe of our bodies. I often sit in meditation just becoming aware of the billions of miracles right inside me. The flowing of blood, the exacting mixture of chemicals to bring nutrients, energy and life, the pumping of the heart, the processing of the brain, breathing, cellular growth, skin replacement, and on and on. I call this divine memory.

Divine memories bring life and remind us of the miracle we all are part of and in fact are!

Chapter 7: July
July 17

Overcome

I was reading a heroes book to my grandson, and Nelson Mandela was the story we read today. Nelson Mandela overcame atrocities without a vengeance and in doing so, was able to overcome human barriers to true love for him and a country!

He was able to use this deep love to heal a nation of people and show the world how we can transcend anything with love at our core!

The lesson for me is that Mandela chose to heal versus be the wound. In the many small atrocities that occur in our lives, we choose to be wounds and in time they build up into a large scab. Scabs stall deep healing, they remind us daily of the wound and enabling us to pick at the scab and relive the pain again and again!

It is a choice to heal, feel the pain and dress the wound rather than pick at it.

Chapter 7: July
July 18

Reflections

How hard is it to look in the mirror and say I love you to yourself? It is pretty hard. Our ego is a master of disguise, sometimes building us into a better person and worthy, and sometimes knocking us down as unworthy.

All the while, our true self hides behind the mirror of reflection. Try every morning for two weeks – to reflect and state your worthiness to your self.

The reflection will get softer and softer.

Chapter 7: July
July 19

Blinking

On average we blink a lot, 1,000 times per day. Blinking opens the mind to intervals of light and dark. If we add up the time we blink, the fractions of a second are pretty small, so despite the 1,000 occurrences, we find ourselves most often in light.

I see this as a pointer to the promise that we come from light with interspersed periods of dark, rather than the other way around. If you can embrace this truth for yourself, it will lift your days more than burden them.

When you perceive a situation coming from light, you will see 'good' in all things labeled bad. This is a divine gift.

When we know there is light in all things, when darkness comes, we will know this too will pass and that knowing will lessen the despair.

Treat every dark period, as a blink knowing in a flash your eyes will see the light. This too shall pass.

Chapter 7: July
July 20

Faith in deep water

I was watching my grandchild's swimming class. Watching a newer swimmer tire is a metaphor of how faith builds.

They wiggle and struggle, as they believe more energy, more trying, keeps them afloat. Then fatigue overcomes them and they need to relax to preserve energy and make it to the end of the pool. In the relaxing, they more easily float to preserve life.

In letting go, we feel lighter and more easily lifted. We can then replenish, and make it to the end of the pool more confidently!

Chapter 7: July
July 21

Revelation

I have never understood the Book of Revelation and in fact always feared it! I have often thought how did this become a book of the Bible?

It confuses me with all the symbolism of death and disaster and I believe it has led many to stray. I have in fact only heard one sermon on revelation, so theologians have difficulty with it as well. But yet in that sermon, Barbara Brown Taylor revealed that in the darkness that seems overwhelming, when all kinds of monsters and creatures come our way...God is still bigger than all that!

When we are faced with more than we can handle, when it seems likely faith is not working nor going to work, when all seems lost, God is still bigger!

Those brave souls who survive the worst that life can throw at us: holocaust survivors, apartheid, POW's, the abused, all know this uniquely. And some have come out singing that God is bigger than that, revealing this truth!

God is not the creator of the worst things we can imagine, He is in there with us, mixing it up, swirling around with all the mayhem and in the end, bigger than anything we can experience.

Chapter 7: July
July 22

Ubuntu

My wife had an Ubuntu day for the young ladies of Sudan. The African term meaning ' I am because you are!' has profound spiritual meaning. We are 'one' has been understood for a long time and alive in global tribal customs. We are essentially relearning what our African brothers knew - that all is connected through universal law, that we as humans co-create and bring life from each other.

This applies not just to people as all of nature is connected. I am because of the trees, I am because of the rain, I am because of my genes, I am because of you. I am inside me!

You will find this deeper meaning in every religious path, it is a pointer that exclaims we are ' one' beyond our comprehension to understand all things! Yet in its simplest form, if I am because you are....how could I hurt you?

Chapter 7: July
July 23

Walk away from pain

Job was a wonderfully faithful man of the Old Testament. He is famous for not giving in when things kept getting worse, he refused to think his God was giving up on him. He struggled mightily.

In the end, he walked away from his grief to find the light. Sometimes we need to just walk away. In the absence of our being in the fight, the fight diminishes. By creating some space, our struggles may just lose their hold on us and fall away because we are not there to hold them up.

Chapter 7: July
July 24

The convertible

I have been in a convertible with the top open only once. It was in NYC and as you may imagine, it opened a world unseen before, with large vertical vistas! I saw the reason for the fascination so many have with convertibles! It was inspiring.

When a convertible converts from roof to no roof, it symbolizes changing from a closed perspective to open wonder. When it is stormy or cold around us, we can put the roof up and protect ourselves, when it is sunny and warm, we open ourselves to the expanse and wonder of the heavens!

As is often the case in our lives, when things are stormy we need to seek comfort, protection and when things are bright and sunny, we seek to rejoice and be glad in it!

All too often though, we have the roof down all the time. We often create our pain because we isolate and close ourselves inside with the roof closed!

We need to seek the wonder and expanse that exists around us more often. We might get wet or cold, but more often than not, we will expose the wonderful expanse of possibilities.

Chapter 7: July
July 25

Light revealed

I play a laser game with our cats. They love to chase the light and often the game is for me to move the light out of their sight so the cats cannot find it.

They sit quietly knowing the light is somewhere and they await the lights coming to pounce once again. All too often, I trick them with the light behind them.

Our lives and God's light work like my cat game. God's light is sometimes hidden behind obstacles that are real of sometimes of our own making!

The game of life sometimes has us so turned around we too are facing the wrong way. The trick is to know the light is there, slow down and look around and over the obstacles. Seek and you shall find.

Chapter 7: July
July 26

When does the wave know its water?

Thich Nhat Hanh is a monk who spends his days reflecting deep parallels about our life and purpose. He says enlightenment for a wave is the moment it realizes it is water.

This is a parallel metaphor for us humans, realizing amongst the sea of humanity we are all one sea and one humanity leading us to being enlightened ourselves.

In feeling that oneness, we become aware we are part of creation, connected like the ocean connects every drop of water. True love comes when we see that we love ourselves when we love all people! True grace comes from knowing and living that truth.

Chapter 7: July
July 27

The golden rule?

I listen to the news of the day and I am dismayed at hearing the hurtful things we do to each other. The golden rule has been distorted suggesting that 'if you do this to me, I will do it to you and others'.

When we are hurt in life, we oft times learn that hurt. Many who were abused, turn to abuse themselves! These are not actions of the spirit.

Anger cannot coexist with faith, hope and love so the light we can bring to our pain will eventually overcome the dark.

In giving love, you will know how you need to be treated.

Chapter 7: July
July 28

The deep breath of healing

Paul Boyle is a trauma healer from Africa who has been helping the traumatized heal all over the world. He once told us that we must care for ourselves intentionally because trauma takes hold of the healer every bit as real and strong as the victimized. It spreads among us if we are not careful. Jesus and Buddha taught us that there is a spirit in us that can allow the pain of others in without turning us into pain.

This is the miracle of healing...to magically breathe into our spirit the pain, offering love and compassion to others, and then breathe out any toxins so we can start again.

The deep breath is necessary for complete healing!

Chapter 7: July
July 29

Bronte and incessant love

Bronte was my one and only dog. She was a beautiful Sheltie, with the most precious face and even a more precious demeanor. She became my soul companion.

If I were to move from one room to another, she would follow and find herself a spot to curl up nearby. Her presence was constant and warming to my soul! If I did not feel her around, I felt an emptiness and would call her to see if she was alright. Within seconds she made herself seen with the face of joyous anticipation - with an expression like "you called".

She was my shadow of light if that is possible? She came to work with me, and she slept in our bed, she drove with me and stayed near at all times of her consciousness. She did this until her age no longer made that possible. She was always there in love.

As her life cycled, some of that changed and our roles changed. Having cancer and 17 years of life behind her made it difficult for her to be ever present in the ways I describe, but I found her and brought her with me as much as I could. I lifted her up and down the steps, lifted her into bed or the car, and when she was not near me, I often looked for a spot near her.

We were together in spirit until she asked to go home to God. I cry now as I write, but in reflection she was not asking to go to God, she was already with God, she was just asking to rest her tired body!

I am grateful for her singular love and for the experience of a love that never ends. I miss her and yet I still feel her, and still receive joy from any thought of her! I know that the world is a better place for her life.

Chapter 7: July
July 30

Writers block

I have never personally experienced writers block but I have a similar experience in managing creativity. When I need to expand my thinking I need the energy of seeing more, feeling the energy of lots of people around, and create a more expansive view to observe things from afar. Like clockwork, my mind opens!

When our paths are blocked in any way, we need to step back and expand our views. In stepping back, we can see more clearly the obstacles blocking where we need to go.

The tree that had fallen blocking love for us can be stepped over or around, the perceived river between us is really a puddle to be walked through, the ocean we perceived in front of us is a lake we can walk around. Any obstacle when perceived from a distance looks different, smaller, manageable, in fact not an obstacle at all.

Seeing in this way opens the path to where we might now go! We move from blocked choices to expansive choices. We can see a path that is easy to start, and we are moving again!

The block was really never there!

Chapter 7: July
July 31

Bring the children

We visited great nieces that celebrated communions in the last two weeks. It brought me to thinking about children and Jesus. He asked for the children to not be hidden as was customary in that day, but to be brought to him. He marveled in their pure faith, their lack of agenda and their playful thoughts. He wished that we would in fact take lessons from them.

We are evolving to unlearn what we have learned as adults to get closer to the purity of a child. Jesus asked us to pay attention to children! Open your eyes in joy for a new day, enjoy recess as your best subject, play hard, fight sleep because every moment is special, know not malice and bias, care to be loved deep enough that it brings you to tears to disappoint others, sleep hard. Oh the lessons available for us all.

Bring the children to me and give me ears to listen, eyes to see and insight to embrace the moment we are in.

Chapter 8: August
August 1

Becoming

I experienced the dark side of life when we received a call that our young Sudanese friend Paul had been shot and killed. He had a tough life in his young 26 years, seeing more of hell on earth than I want to even acknowledge.

He was becoming though. He was two years sober and drug free, he just finished a CNA class, attending school and planning a trip to Africa to see his mom for the first time since he was 8 years old. He was just blossoming with a wisdom that only God could impart and that made us feel like he was becoming what God had designed. His early life was like a flower being forced to open too soon! He left his mom and dad at 8 years of age, being told he would be safer in a refugee camp far from home. He grew up without parents and then was sent to America at 14 as an unaccompanied minor. The lovely flower that was to be Paul was prematurely opened and in doing so, the delicate petals were ripped and created some damage.

He was now just acknowledging that he was a child of God, and that his wounded petals could be fixed! You can't rush such growth. Paul used to tell us that until he decided to grow inside, there was no changing him from the outside.

Becoming is a beautiful thing.

Chapter 8: August
August 2

The depths of our own story

Yeats poem on mermaids tells of the mermaid hugging her human loved one and joyfully plunging down in the sea, not realizing her lover would drown in her environment.

The mermaid failed to see that her life and her lover's life could not survive solely in one world.

We too need to understand our own perspectives are never enough when sharing with another person. We need compassion enough to understand another's perspective as every bit as important and right as ours! Where do they come from, how do they perceive the very same things we do and then, in a ' deep listening' find true understanding of their perspective.

If this is possible, we will create a wonderful bridge of common ground from which to grow together.

Chapter 8: August
August 3

Our dweller is eternal

The Bhagavad-Gita states that our bodies are perishable, but inside, the dweller is eternal. This part of the Hindu holy book positions our spirits existing as an energy for eternity, only inhabiting our bodies for this short time on earth. The word perishable paints a picture of our bodies holding our spirits temporarily, like the skin of a fruit holds the inner sweetness.

In all faiths, we are brought to this perspective that our holy spirit is within and eternal, if we can reach that space and know this is true of all people or even sentient beings, we will find truer peace.

Chapter 8: August
August 4

Dark thoughts

I know a young woman whose mind is constantly chattering stories and it cannot easily be quieted. Her ego plays the grand screenwriter and director to present fabricated truth all the time to protect her in some way.

We all have this at some level where our ego builds a story; we become judge and jury, we build ourselves up, we form false attachments. We create a false self! We live often in this fabricated world without realizing it is not real!

At the same time, we imagine a future that is not real, we imagine being less than we are, and we create worry.

All this chatter keeps us from embracing the present moment as it truly is! I have come to be fully aware of stories I weave that are not based on absolute truth and they will create a 'me' that I don't want to become if I believe those thoughts.

The 'imagined' thoughts wash away under that scrutiny of absolute truth. Katie Byron calls this the 4 questions. What thoughts are you conjuring at this moment that is not 'absolutely' true? Who would you be without them? What light can you bring to those dark thoughts so they are washed away? In the end, less chatter and more truth will bring a peace. It will settle you into what really is happening and bring you to engage in that truth right at this moment.

When engaged in the moment, we are most with God and most happy!

Chapter 8: August
August 5

The chick birth

My grandson's class just received eggs to incubate in the next 21 days! I did some research with him about the birth process for chicks. The way the chicks finally enter our world got me to thinking about the parallels to our own experience!

Like all creatures, the chick follows instincts and the natural path towards its birth. We know and do nothing before we are born except participate somehow in the miracle. The chick panics a bit in that as it grows too big for the egg, it's only way out is to eat its protective shell because it is growing too large and has no more food! At one point, with its world as it knows it falling apart literally, exhausted, it falls through the shell - and is born!

At that heightened moment of despair and worry of the unknown, when its white shell sky is literally cracking and falling, a new world appears and they are born to a new life!

I can liken this process to any of life's major transformations; where God's hand is guiding events more than we know.   We need to relax in faith, and be born to a new opportunity.

Even death, our last and greatest transformation, is divinely designed and letting go might be a path to another birth!   We fear death because of the unknown, but was there anything to fear in the birth process when we just were? I wonder if death is just another guided miracle where we are breaking through our shell and falling through death to be born again?

From the other side it must look so natural, so peaceful, so embracing, so awe filled!

Chapter 8: August
August 6

The agony and the ecstasy

The old wide world of sports show had as its slogan, 'the ecstasy of winning and the agony of defeat'. Is life really so black and white? With time behind me, and with experiences all over the agony and the ecstasy spectrum, I see the difference as ever so slight and not as the polar opposites expressed in that slogan.

Take the world-class athlete, running a race where the difference between winning and losing is often hundredths of seconds. This is not a polar opposite, but yet in an Olympic race, someone won global glory and someone did not.

Can we look at these opposite emotions for basically the same performance not as an either or, but as a 'both and!' We both won and lost! In the material world we sometimes lose sight of the impermanence of glory and the impermanence of defeat.

In such times, if we can see winning and losing as closer to one, we emerge our experience a better person.

August 7

De clutter

In our western lives, we accumulate. It is a value of our society to have things, show them off so to speak. Letting go of things helps us become more of our true selves because we drop false attachments.

We do this with thoughts and memories too, accumulating them as gifts that we store and show off, or pains we store and hide. We have a full house inside our minds. It feels hard to throw anything away or give up on old ways of thinking or feeling, but if we don't do so we run the risk we can't take on anymore!

Let some things go and see how it feels.

August 8

A cat's sleep

Our cats sleep a wonderful sleep, peaceful, no cares, and a complete release of the day's stresses.

If only we had that skill, our lives would be better for it. Release all worries, surrender to no thing, seek rest and come out renewed.

August 9

Random

Mark Nepo identified an early meaning of the word 'random' to be that moment when a horse's four hooves are off the ground. I liken that definition with the infinitesimal spaces of our lives that are nearly ever noticed! There are spaces that fill us daily though they are not easily or readily observable to our conscious minds.

The natural spaces between breathing in and out, or the heart bringing blood in and then pushing blood out are holy spaces that beckon us every second but get lost in their reliability. Too often we take them for granted. Should they fail or sputter - oh boy, do we pay attention!

Life's random moments are often thought to be outside our knowing control, but when you ponder them, are they not just moments we were not paying attention to or taking for granted?

The hummingbird, the emergence of sunshine, a breathtaking vista, beautiful music, these are all holy spaces lost to our busy mind. The decision to tune in and allow our selves to pay attention and even stay awhile in those holy moments is seminal to being more Holy. In those spaces of divine beckoning, the path can change us. Follow it!

Chapter 8: August
August 10

Running

I saw runners today, running in an organized event for charity. As I drove, I commented to my wife that they all were struggling and not one looked like they were runners!

I laughed a bit, but later sat in wonder thinking what were they running for or from? It was not social, as most we passed were alone. It was likely not for fun, as most looked pained and not fit!

I realized that life itself was running. In this race, each had their own unique cause or pain that brought them forward. Running for MS, running for Aunt Sue with cancer, running away from your own pain. At the same solitary time, they were in communion; Running together, being cheered on by water stations along the way or cars that tooted encouragement.

These runners found a will to go beyond and at the end of the day, exhausted yet accomplished, their will was merged with their cause, their love was lifted for another, or their pain was subsumed by the 'communion' of the 'run'.

Life is a metaphorical run when you just can't run anymore, run!

Chapter 8: August
August 11

Find your voice

I love listening to the sounds of life. I frequently go to a coffee shop to be around chatter. It livens my own mind to be among the crowds of people who are engaged.

Our voices are a sacred gift, allowing us to express ourselves to the joys and sorrows of living and reconcile our true selves. Our voices left free, express our inner selves to others. I wonder how life's pressures suppress that voice over time. I see it drag many down.

We need to find our inner voices to have any chance of expression of our inner self and a full life that that infers! Can you imagine the bird not singing, the dancer not dancing or the musician not playing?

We are "not", unless our voice is free!

Chapter 8: August
August 12

The rock of Alcatraz

We lived in SanFrancisco in the 1980s and visited the maximum security prison Alcatraz many times with guests. It strikes me now how often we would view the 'rock' from shore at the same time we viewed seal island, another rock in the ocean that was a safe haven for seals. The seals clumsily found their way to the rock to escape the constant tumult of the tides and the waves! They collapsed together, exhausted, finding a peace amongst the other seals there for the same reason. They lay together and found rest from the storm, a camaraderie of oneness.

In a funny way, they found what many of wounded humans find in a safe haven...a place for us to be our true selves, safe from the barrage of the day and protected by fellow warriors! Whether we are wounded or prisoners in some symbolic or real way, we need to find our own safe haven amongst loved ones to fully recover, heal and renew!

Chapter 8: August
August 13

Eagle scouts - Be prepared

Our dear friends son Jack received his eagle scout. In his words of acceptance he said his Eagle project taught him the power of preparedness. Of course the scout slogan is 'be prepared', so I was taken by the coincidence of the truth.

In the spirit versus our physical worlds, we are prepared by not being prepared! Often things we would rather avoid, like death or failure, bring new life and renewal.

In our physical experience of failure, death brings new ideas, new perspectives, and new compassion to forge renewal.

So preparedness works in a paradox. It can come from diligence and planning and it can come in faith and it almost always comes in disguise.

Chapter 8: August
August 14

Help

Father Tom Keating is the creator of contemplative prayer. This is a process of connection to the one God with us through an open meditative heart!

Keating says the shortest and perhaps most powerful prayer is to merely say 'help'! Asking for something we need creates the vulnerability that lets God into our spirits. And in the end, that is the answer to all prayers.

To know you are held up by something so much larger than yourself.
God help me!

Chapter 8: August
August 15

Humbled in majesty

When you think of the wonders of the world, people come from all ends of the earth to just stand amongst the wonder. It is there that we know we are part of a much larger universe, we know there is a creator who is larger than our tiny minds can grasp, and we are humbled.

Being humble brings us to our roots. Humbled from the root word humus means the soil. The soil connects us with all things older and natural. There is a peace in being close to the soil that farmers and gardeners alike have discovered. Humus provides us perspective outside our small worries to grander designs of the one God.

In that insight we are humbled and when we are humbled, we know all is good!

Chapter 8: August
August 16

All I know versus all I am

My wife and I are struggling with the way our life has turned as we enter our last years. We are finding it difficult to adapt to the pressures of aging and new stresses that are coming our way from parent's health to our grand children's needs.

Many things that were easy in the early years are now hard. Many dreams are slowed. I want to fix it all and make it better.

What I have learned is that we all live in an expansive and then contracting world whether we pay attention or not. If there is an elixir it appears to be to accept the process as natural and to move with it versus resist it.

Eckhart Tolle speaks about the rhythm of all things and the contraction cycle is as beautiful as the expansion cycle.

The breathing out carries with it toxins we release, and leaves us empty at its end, but it is not a complete breath without it. In that cycle of grace we are at peace and it is not all that I know that brings joy to this time, it is all that 'I am'!

Chapter 8: August
August 17

Not getting what we want

I sometimes feel the pain of loss of a life I had once lived. I worry about life more and my assigned roles, such as grandparent, son, husband seem to be more complicated.

Sometimes in the midst of worry, I yearn for more or regret where I am.

When we face these issues, we best look to wonder.
Metaphors like the thousands of seeds strewn on the ground, or the thousands of fish eggs laid that really create but a few but glorious wonders, teach us to look for more opportunities to discover ourselves in the endless possibilities.

We can spend time in remorse that the one egg or the one seed we cherished did not make it but in doing so, we lose sight of the endless joy and wonder that life offers us regardless of when.

Focusing one-way is despair, the other wonder. The choice is ours to make at every juncture. The life I had is the same life I have, the possibilities as open and glorious as my choices. We need to be open to the possibilities and embrace each life segment with the openness to learn what it is teaching me!

There is so much wonder around us we should be in awe every day.

August 18

Be settled

My mother in law always wanted her son to be settled. I always wondered what that really meant to her. I envision being settled like a rock settling in a seabed. Nestled tightly, protected, watching the world float by with no cares.

Seng-Ts'an writes 'be serene in the oneness of things and erroneous views disappear by themselves'. This is what I view as being settled! Firmly nestled and watching things sort of float by.

I want to be settled like that, firm in my position, safe, watching the world float by. We then can appreciate all that is around us and be one with it for as long as it stays in our company, but knowing that won't be for long, but ok with that premise.

In most times we are happiest when we do not attach or cling to things that float by. Joy in the moment is natural when you are firmly settled enjoying each one while you are one with it.

August 19

The pursuit of happiness

Thomas Jefferson had divine guidance in his words and insights. When you delve deeper into his key phrase commending to all people's the 'pursuit' of happiness, not happiness...is a truth revealed to me!

One cannot just be happy without the journey. The pursuit reveals happiness because by its definition it lives through strife and sadness, insight and joy. Happiness is about 'being' through all moments. That is the true pursuit.

August 20

The movement of grace

My wife joined me at a conference for trauma healing. Our late friend Chol was supposed to be on a panel called 'a foot in both worlds' before his life was taken. We were late so we stood in the back of the ballroom with 450 people seated listening to the morning keynote.

I went for a tea and when I returned Ann Marie had a young man standing next to her. As it turned out, the unexplainable yet real movement of Gods grace was in evidence. This young man was nervously waiting his time for a panel discussion.

He was replacing a friend who was killed last month. He was Chol's replacement! To Ann Marie he was a holy visit from Chol, coming to her in an impossible set of timing and place coincidences only possible with God. It is evidence that the movement of grace is there always!

I can liken the movement of Gods grace to the ocean tides. We, like fish are within the tide, and influenced by it, and mysteriously apart and contained at the same time. Each moment in our life includes the power to see grace, sometimes it's so strong we are forced to see and be changed by it, sometimes life itself is so strong we are pushed by as if grace did not exist.

Grace Is there in every interaction and importantly, there in every 'almost' interaction...the ones we don't begin because we rushed by or turned our attention elsewhere! Our purpose is to tune in more and be led by the grace of God.

Chapter 8: August
August 21

Can you see others feelings?

Like many others, I rush through life too often and as a result I miss much. As the TV show of my youth used as its tag line, 'There are 8 million stories in the naked city', and I don't know but a handful!

I am not even sure I know my own story!

Jesus had this capability of seeing others feelings. He was so tuned into another that he could sense their burdens, their pains and seek to heal them. He emitted love from his soul to another's. To live our purpose, we need to open ourselves to the stories around us and see another's feelings.

Can you imagine the healing power that would exist if we each had a bubble over our head with our burdens and joys written for others to see and react too? How much more would we be able to help, or pray or intercede for good!

Those bubbles are there if we care to look.

August 22

Building a fence

I was thinking about building a fence around our Peter Rabbit vegetable garden to keep unwanted rabbits out! I was designing the foolproof fence! Then I thought in life do fences really work to plan?

In our lives, we build imaginary fences that are more foolproof then even can be conjectured by our real fences? We don't let others in, and we don't let our pains out. If our pains are locked inside without escape, and our true selves sit outside with no ability to be fed or nurtured by the garden inside, we are both imprisoned and hopeless.

Fences that are foolproof are for fools. Let the rabbits be rabbits!

August 23

Bringing love to our life

There is always just one moment in which we are intended to bring our fullest attention and love. So, why don't we?

The next moment per se comes from that first interaction so in effect we create our next moment. That series of now moments is God's plan. If taken in love, you will have a new path and journey more love filled.

When we are in this moment in fear, the opposite happens.   In these cases, the next moment grows differently without love as its center and God's plan is deferred or derailed. Love will not be as frequent.

God gives us chances again in the next moment to create a different outcome by bringing love versus fear. With enough experience, we will want to be and stay more in the moment of love, and bring our own light to the world.

August 24

Be not afraid

I love the words to the Christian song "Be not afraid, I go before you always, come follow me, I will give you rest".

Worry is a major part of our fears manifest. Our thoughts bring us to places that are not real, yet they bring real fear! Being in the moment with 'what is' regardless of the pain that is present, brings the potential to heal and to be full of joy.

When we are most vulnerable, grace is most real!
Be not afraid, I go before you always -- Go rest.

Chapter 8: August
August 25

Step over obstacles

My dad's Parkinson's disease is progressing and leaving him with less and less mobility. His mind is strong, so his depth of despair grows. He finds it limiting to use his walker because his legs fail to move!

We ordered a new walker that has a laser beam attached to the back wheels. The beam serves to trick the brain by creating an imaginary step -- hoping to enable my dad to lift the leg to avoid tripping over the imaginary obstacle. With each lift over the obstacle we achieve a step, and freedom!

In life, we face these obstacles and often they are not as real as we make them out to be. If we could trick our brain to step over them they would likely soften or even disappear. Often, our own thoughts present these obstacles. They create worry or self esteem issues and if we can 'step over that thought' we would move more toward freedom!

Chapter 8: August
August 26

We are what we are

I imagine and daydream often, usually I dream of being something or somewhere different than who I am and where I am.

I have found that the answers to those dreams are already in us as we are already whole and loved and in fact perfect in Gods eyes. Accepting and embracing that is a key to happiness.

Your dreams and reality are not ever far apart.   So, reflect on your gifts, create gratitude for what you already have, know you are capable of having fun, you are living joyfully, you are Gods precious gift!

Then, no matter how big your dreams or how big the gaps, you will realize that in reality you are already whole, who you are, and where you need to be!

Chapter 8: August
August 27

Grace filled movements

We move through life looking for control of everything. We think too much, we plan to much, we worry too much.

Among nature, we see something different. The grace filled capability to be at one with God, to go with the flow is everywhere!
Birds soar on the invisible wind trusting it will be there, fish move to the invisible streams or the powers of the tide. This is the divine movement of grace.

We too can be open to the movement of grace by opening ourselves to the invisible force around us, let it guide us every bit as gracefully and peacefully as the birds and fish and bring wonder and peace to our lives.

In that grace, we become one with God and the answers to all life's questions will be left at our feet. We too can move in grace.

Chapter 8: August
August 28

Freeing pain

We often create our own health problems by holding pain inside. It is a paradox of a sort that our instinct is to hold pain aside to protect ourselves and yet that creates more pain.

Facing and feeling our pains is the only way we free ourselves of the pain. In that hard work, of addressing what really pains us, we can chip away at the false walls we have built to protect us. With each pain freed from hurting us again, we free our souls a bit more.

A freed soul rejoices!

Chapter 8: August

August 29

Sliding doors

There is a great movie called 'sliding doors' that shows the power of moving through each moment with more intention. Just one slight change in our current moment ripples through the next and is so powerful that it literally impacts the path of our life.

The movie artfully tracked two parallel courses of one life, based on the minute detail of making a train or not! It is enlightening and frightful to know how powerful each moment can be.

If we could embrace that truth, we would treasure it, engage it and embrace it more fully.

So why not?

Chapter 8: August
August 30

Arriving

Letting go of your plan

I have read of college kids who go to Europe for a summer abroad without a plan. They buy a train pass and then go! There is a level of spiritual destiny in a plan without a destination or timeline. It opens each moment to be savored and then used to create where the next moment may take us, we are never late, nor lost! We are always where we are meant to be! That is as close to Gods plan as I can conceive!

Each moment becomes part of the plan and we savor it more, stay with it with more intention and reveal Gods purpose for us at each point.

Let go of your plan and see what happens.

Chapter 8: August
August 31

Quiet teachers everywhere

We often think of ourselves as being in charge of ourselves. Our life experience has taught us we are in control.

Then one day we are stuck; depressed, sick, or deeply worried and we are lost. When stuck badly enough, we will give up out of fatigue or let go; in those times we are more likely to find the teachers sent by God to help us.

They are everywhere and revealed in mystical ways; a chance meeting, a stumble, a letter, a sign. When we are a ready and willing student, Quiet teachers abound.

Seek and Listen.

Chapter 9: September
September 1

The miracles before us

We experienced a miracle of nature today that was freeing for our spirits. Our baby wrens, which were nested on our front porch, were taught to fly today by their mom and dad.

All of a sudden the babies left the nest and under the close tutelage of their parents attempted to fly. It was amazing watching them leap and flap, and make progress slowly. At one point I took our camera and started a video from our porch, where one baby remained trying to figure out what they needed to do to fly!

Suddenly, mom and dad showed up, called another baby to their side and asked them both to be still to protect them from me. All was just quiet. What an amazing thing to witness!!

Then mom came behind me and started yelling at me to leave. Once I did, they returned to their flight training and eventually the family flew to a new home! We were in awe and felt uplifted to so closely witness one of nature's miracles.

In contemplating this, I recognize miracles are everywhere, among animals, birds, flowers, trees, even people! We don't need to be hit by a major miracle to stop and take note.

If we can take a deep breath at any given moment and become aware, we can marvel in each one of those miracles that surround us all the time -- we would sit in awe continuously, and be more grateful for our life.

What a joyous way to live.

Chapter 9: September
September 2

Imaging and sacred visits

When I played baseball, I used imaging often and to great success. I wasn't alone as it seemed commonplace amongst our team. I was often anticipating the next play and executing how it was envisioned. I remember distinctly one play.

We were playing a championship level game in Dalton, Massachusetts against a team that had a number one major league draftee. His name was Gino Quirk. I remember he could run as fast as we had seen, but yet hit with great power. As he stepped to the plate his first time, I envisioned readying myself for a ball hit to me. I then saw a vision right before the pitch, he would bunt toward me.

I envisioned sprinting to the ball and in one fluid motion, snatch the ball and throw to first just in time to get the speedy wunderkind! Gino swung and the ball trickled down the third base line. I was ready and already in motion seemingly one step ahead of the real time action. I knew exactly how the play was to evolve, I executed the way I saw it in my mind and reflex handled the rest!

Imaging works in any circumstance in our lives, sometimes we tune in and sometimes we don't. I see imaging now as a holy visitation, where our God brings us value and insights to ponder, reflect upon and grow. We need to give these sacred visits their due, take the time to both embrace and encourage them and our lives will be richer for the taking. Each image depicts a potential new path to take and where it leads only God knows!

Chapter 9: September
September 3

God around us

My African friend Paul is a former priest serving God in new ways. He often prays with a preface that touches me deeply. "to God before us, behind us, Above us and below us, to our right and to our left." It is a wonderful prayer of God visually protecting us from every side, and I now add 'and God inside us' as I know now that God placed a seed within as the Holy Spirit.

The Holy Spirit is our protector from the obstacles we encounter in living a pure and spirit filled life! Ralph Waldo Emerson's poem states 'what lies behind us and before us are tiny matters when compared to what lies inside us'.

Pray to the God who lives inside us, and outside us -- to our left and right, before us and behind us, above us and below us! There is no limit to our greatness when we feel protected in this way and can step out in faith!

Chapter 9: September
September 4

Who is watching?

I marvel at seeing differences within children when they know they are being watched. Our 3 year old grandchild is a master at escaping the watch. She finds a way to move out of sight and before you know it, she is exploring something she should not be exploring. When called she reappears with that look of ' I have not been trouble making'!

Have you ever thought who is watching us and how often? I often have conversations with myself when considering a next step. Don't take that chocolate, pick up that trash, stop at the stop sign! I have come to know my 'real self' from those conversations and they have convinced me that I am watching myself!

I believe this happens to us all. Said another way, our true spiritual self is watching our ego and false self! In the awareness of this alone we diminish the ego's strength and we enable our true self to emerge.

.
Chapter 9: September
September 5

The balance to walk

Why do we stumble?

I reflected for a long time on "stumbling". Why despite good intention do we stumble so often?

While doing an in-depth study on stumbling under the guidance of a spiritual director, I witnessed our grandchild started walking for the first time. How symbolic as I watched a pure spirit struggle with real stumbling! Each time she becomes self conscious, and starts to think, she loses focus and falls.

Do we stumble for the same reasons? When we think too much, or get caught up in 'what ifs', we lose focus and sometimes lose our way. When lost, stumbling is inevitable. When my grandchild stumbled, unburdened by the fear of being wrong, she just got back up and started anew!

How we react is so much more important than the stumble. Get up and start anew!

Chapter 9: September
September 6

No man

I was reading a graphic novel with my grandson. The Kung Fu expert trained the books protagonists in the martial arts. He would not however grant them a black belt until they knew who was the greatest man in the world. After many wrong answers and much thinking, they finally understood the inner truth of the question and the answer was 'no man'. This happens to be the Buddha's definition of himself and us all!

When we consider ourselves no man, we create a gift of spirit. We recognize that we are both all nothing and all God. We are not better than any other being and not worse. We find more truth because we understand the relative naming of all things as transient. Living life as 'no man' is living a fuller life!

Chapter 9: September
September 7

Expect good things

I have been saying to my grandson to expect good things each morning on the way to school. I sometimes ask him what good things happened today and in his desire to find something that pleases me, he looks to deeper thoughts such as "hugging me when I got home, having dinner together, helping a classmate".

I have been criticized for expecting too many good things myself! I have learned though that the expectation of finding something leads to the finding! Sometimes this is called the law of abundance.

So, in a real way, the expectation brings the expected.

Chapter 9: September
September 8

Can you wait?

As we go through times of despair or hurt, waiting for it to pass rather than doing something is a real challenge! Our human nature is to want to fix the broken.

Most things are impermanent and therefore will move on and change. As we recognize the truth in that, we will more often see our worries smooth away in time.

Eckhart Tolle tells the story of the wisdom teacher who answers "is that so?" to both every bad situation and every good situation he confronts! Over time he does not over react to good news that blesses him and the bad news that confronts him. He remains calm and aware of all things around him...this too shall pass is his first embrace. In the end he is happiest with his unchanging spirit and let's go of the twists and turns of the world.

All things are impermanent and the better we understand that the more comfortable we can be in waiting.

Chapter 9: September
September 9

De-clutter

The old sage invites these learned men to tea. After a brief discussion, the sage pours their tea and despite the fact the teacup is overflowing, he keeps pouring.

The learned men react confused, and the sage merely says 'your minds are like this teacup, they are full and nothing can get in'.

How can we see wonder, experience stillness or feel joy when nothing can get in? We need spaces to live life and experience life to its fullest.

To create space, we need to be empty! Emptiness can be physical and mental. Removing clutter from your physical space is every bit as important as removing the clutter of your mind. God needs space to work.

Chapter 9: September
September 10

Hatred

On this eve of 9/11 we sit innocently, yet September 11th will live with us our whole life. This singular event of evil lives, from the economic collapse it caused, to the loss of innocence. So in all things evil, where is the good that comes through redemption?

Is this not an event and a place where God's redemption should be so clear? Has God had enough time and chances to redeem this ugliness? Perhaps we are too busy to see the changes occurring or more likely too caught up in revenge or anger so that our own evil hides the redemption.

I have come to understand that in all things, God needs partners. In extreme hatred, He waits for us to 'see' our own hatred first as one not redeemed cannot see redemption. I wait in faith, I pray for my own redemption and for my eyes to be open to the opportunities already waiting!

Chapter 9: September
September 11

How do we learn?

Confucius confuses me.

He stated we become our true self through understanding and he calls that our culture. Yet he goes on to say we can arrive at understanding from being our true self - and he calls that nature. That is a circuitous argument to me!

The trap is that nature and environment are not mutually exclusive and they are circuitous.

We have to be open to the spirit at all times to find our true self. For example, If we rush by a bird singing or a glorious sunset, or if we engaged in meaningless anger in response to our daily experience, we miss being our true self.

So, the truth of the Confucian message may be that we need to create space to 'see' the spirit in all things (natural and experiential) and only then we will truly integrate and see.

Chapter 9: September
September 12

Reflecting God

I am most in wonder when I am outside at night, a full moon lights our way and the universe miraculously sits in space!

The moon reflects so much light that although it is not the source in a way it becomes the source for me and others who need light.

Similarly, we can reflect the light of God. Our personal light is a reflection of how much of God we bring to the moment! The stronger that connection, the more light we reflect, the more soothing we are to those around us!

In a way, we serve as a moon in our universe, a reflector of the God within and a light for many to see through their darkness.

Chapter 9: September
September 13

Ducks

Ducks are graceful creatures, yet, so much is going on beneath the surface of the water. We are the same.

When seeming peaceful we have similar frenetic thoughts running in our minds. Our face to the world is often so different than how we feel. Our mind chatter can be incessant and our thoughts can overwhelm our true self.

Our peace becomes real if we can work to slow the chatter beneath the surface!

Chapter 9: September
September 14

Finding Nemo

We saw a stage story in Disney last week about Nemo. It was beautifully done and got me thinking about fish. Fish glide so easily by moving their little fins and opening and closing their gills to 'breathe'. Nature creates a way for those gills to magically transform their experience of living in water. In essence it is like breathing in water and transforming that water into air to survive and live in their environment.

We can learn from the fish in that we can transform our experiences and live more easily. How often do we take pain and heartache and transform that into wonder and joy? If we could learn to take those experiences and transform them, to look for the good overall, we too can be like Nemo and live more easily, seek adventure and enjoy our life.

Chapter 9: September
September 15

Telling stories

We marvel at our Sudanese friends. When they are together they spin stories for hours. We believe they tell stories of the sacrifices and hardships of their life. In a way we believe the stories bring healing.

Telling stories is an important healing feature of being human and through ancient times it was the only way to teach next generations. The telling over and over again reveals meaning, builds truth and helps us cope.
Imagine the stories of tribal leaders teaching lessons handed down. Imagine the lessons of Saint Paul and how he came closer and closer to Jesus with each telling of his conversion story. Or ancient peoples stories of Buddha or Lao T'su and how those stories kept the healing lessons alive!

In a similar way, our own stories of coping and hope need to be told to forge their meaning on our own hearts and the hearts of others. In the telling we become stronger, we pass down, and in the telling we help form and heal.

Chapter 9: September
September 16

Out with old, in with the new

Our wonderful brains enable memory and most of us have good and bad memories that can be recalled. Sometimes those bad memories haunt us, we recall too much, and our thoughts keep hurting us.

The chambered nautilus lives a model of change in nature that we can reflect upon when considering the hurt caused by old memories. As life happens they grow new chambers and leave the old behind to live in the newest chamber. The old chambers are filled with a gas never to be visited again!

So, they live in the new moment and leave the past behind.

The natural design is one to take note of.

Chapter 9: September
September 17

Lazy Susan ?

We never had a lazy Susan when growing up! I enjoyed using them at restaurants partly because of the novelty and partly because of their usefulness!

Imagine turning a need into fulfillment so easily? Need ketchup turn the lazy Susan and there it is! Need love? Compassion? Listening? If only it were so easy?

Life offers too much false packaging for the Lazy Susan to work in our lives.
Be true to yourself first and then in all relationships.
True happiness waits.

Chapter 9: September
September18

God calling.

The old folklore about a man stranded on a roof in a massive flood beseeching
God to help him speaks to Gods' way of dealing through life's daily interactions.

The story goes on like this... First came a boat, the man declined their help
looking for God. Then a helicopter hovered and again the man declined looking
for God. The waters continued the rise and the man died. In heaven he asked
God whether he heard his cries and where He was? God replied , 'I sent a boat
and a helicopter, what else could I do?'

God calls us to listen and engage in every day interactions, because that is
where He abides. Every interaction is either a door that we open to deeper truth
or one that we gloss over on our way to the next thing on our list.

In staying with a moment rather than glossing over it, we will better see and
serve our Godly purpose. In that minor change of intention, we will see larger
changes in our path, our plans, our life.

Chapter 9: September
September 19

Sacred moments

Growth is something we all strive for, yet in nature growth just happens. There is
no striving!

Our humanness tells us we always need to be reaching for new heights, seeking
new lands, achieving new levels, evolving! Our spirit is different, it seeks it's own
level like waters seeking the lowest point. Spirit seeks to explore what is now,
where you are with no expectations of changing anything.

The Spirit creates sacred moments just where we are and when we strive for
more, we miss the wonder all around us.

Chapter 9: September
September 20

The convergence into one...ultimate truth

The end game of those who study the depths of all sacred texts is pretty much the same. They all have us arrive at the spot that speaks to our oneness! There is one universe of which we are an integral part along with all things and there is one sacred universal leader or spirit or being. Words don't work in naming our God because there are limitations of words that get in the way.

Getting to that one singular truth brings a joy and a peace that passes all understanding!

Why is the human journey along these same paths to truth so hard? Why not have all things work on earth as it is in heaven?

Chapter 9: September
September 21

Just be

Consider becoming more like nature because we are part of all things.
Let's become the flower, the tree, or the dog.

Like the flower we can sit graciously fragile, breathe in the life giving rays of the sun and drink of the soil for nourishment.
Like the tree, we can breathe in the toxic carbon dioxide and breathe out life giving oxygen.
Like the dog we can sit with the sacred moments of just being alongside another, and living the joy of reuniting even if separated for a short time.

If we can move with the grace of life, comforted in knowing all is well like the flower, the tree or the dog, we would worry no more, we would just be.

Chapter 9: September
September 22

Sacred questions?

I know there are sacred questions, and like the game jeopardy they come from sacred answers! Take a moment to live a memory of joy. Holding an infant to bring comfort, viewing the wonder of nature, sharing the pure joy of a child.

These are sacred answers.

Chapter 9: September
September 23

Learning when we are ready

In our constant striving forward, we miss the lessons of the spirit. It is not accepted to seek stillness, to stay awhile in a moment, to just listen, to not have a plan.

We are so full of to-do's there is no room for anything else.

If God comes in the still spaces we create, we need to be ready now.

Chapter 9: September
September 24

Fumbling

I sometimes feel I can't get out of my own way. Despite recognition of our human frailties, and our spiritual promise I find myself falling back into my humanness all too often and in doing so, I fall into some level of despair.

That ongoing fumbling that greets us all is a marker of our humanness. It provides the insight that we are most often only momentarily whole, and will never be fully whole.

We need to live that paradox. Acceptance of our limitations helps us rebound more effectively and catch more glimpses of the light as we journey through our rare and imperfect lives together.

Chapter 9: September
September 25

Consideration

What is the right balance between seeking stillness and considering what life has to offer and why are they not the same?

This is not so clear! There is a story of the Hindu sage who sprung from his morning prayers and shooed his apprentices into the village to live life versus considering life! Jesus more often was ministering versus praying. Like the balance point of a lever, we need to find what is the right balance for us.

In stillness and prayer we find what we need to do and in doing, we do. We can move mountains.

Chapter 9: September
September 26
Forgiving

The origin of this word forgiving is to GIVE FOR!

To give and receive! We tend to miss the lesson that forgiveness is not about the person who hurt us but more about relieving the hurt we put upon ourselves! To forgive is to give us inner freedom rather than an excusing of another's behavior.

The lessons of nature show us this. The animal deals with stress by shaking it off and moving on as if nothing has happened. Ever watch two ducks fighting for food or another's affection? After the quick fight, they flap their wings and then engage each other as if nothing happened. Or an even simpler example comes from disturbing the water with a large stone, it's ripples soon disappear and all remains calm! So the lesson of nature and the ancient wisdom of words align, "give for" the benefits of receiving more yourself when you give...when you forgive, you give yourself a gift!

Chapter 9: September
September 27

Panic

Few of us can see ourselves when in full panic mode! We are in such a heightened state that we react only.

However, if we can step back and observe the situation and our reactions, the panic begins to diffuse. Why? That act of awareness is our conscious "being" observing our ego in action. When this happens, we have the ability to reduce the panic and bring calm.

We can step back because our true self is observing not panicking. We can think more clearly and reduce the stress.

Have you ever played with Chinese handcuffs? The solution in removing the handcuffs demonstrates this point. When you struggle to remove the cuffs by pulling harder and harder, the cuffs tighten and you begin to panic. Only when we stop and observe what is happening do we see that if we lean our fingers into the cuffs without the struggle, do they release their hold!

Chapter 9: September
September 28

Put it down – let it go

I have taken a few Qi Gong courses, the ancient Chinese martial arts program.

One of the poignant lessons of Qi Gong is a dance move that replicates emptying your clenched fist. It is based on ancient wisdom that reflects the story of trapping a monkey by putting food in a jug with a small opening. The monkey reaches in with open hand and grabs the food. With the clenched fist, he cannot get his hand out of the jug and then he struggles not willing to give up the food, he remains trapped caught by his own limitations. Only when he let's go - can he be freed!

We need to do the same metaphorically releasing our pain. If we hold on tight, we will carry it everywhere and remain caught by our own limitations! If we can let it go, we free ourselves.

Chapter 9: September
September 29

Oppression

There are times in ones life when we are faced with the seriousness of confronting real oppression.

The last weeks, one of our dear female friends from Sudan was left behind in a remote village: passports taken, no money, no clothes and worse, they were considered property of her husbands family with 3 small children who were physically and emotionally unprepared for the difficulty of life 'without'.

I witnessed the spirit of a small group of women who chose to involve themselves and overcome huge odds to bring this family back. It was a journey of improbable success with no communications possible to that remote village, limiting the discovery of what happened and what was needed.

Yet, a miracle occurred and this women called for help. The spirit engaged with a vengeance. Remarkably, because one of her children was so sick she was able to leave the village to walk to the nearest clinic for care perhaps a days walk. She borrowed a phone, remembered phone numbers and called.

The spirit guides all such movements in our lives...there are repetitions like this everyday in our lives as others seek help, but less directly. They don't expressly call like our friend, or express at all, yet there is so much need.

We all seek comfort from what oppresses us, what holds us back, what limits us too.

We need to be open to receive or give the call for help. We need to be open to the movement of grace around us so that the spirit acts through us and we open our hearts. We need to say yes to support another and we need to say yes when another seeks to support us! God does great things through us!

Chapter 9: September
September 30

The grass is greener

One of our human traits to dream often works against us! Many dwell on unhappiness by dreaming we can move somewhere else and be happy, or find someone else to be happy.

This is a cursed element of our humanness because we only can find happiness where we are embracing who we are. Our recourse to unhappiness is not to run or hide or move, but to sit still and open our hearts

Chapter 10: October
October 1

The leaf in a stream

While walking, I stopped at an overpass that has a stream below and I watched what the stream carried by.

So effortlessly items give their trust to the stream and they float worry free, twisting around rocks, down mini falls and around logs. It was all so effortless.

I noticed a fragile leaf make its way around every barrier. It seems that having full faith is like being a leaf in the stream.

When we are placed in the universal stream of Gods' grace, we too can float consciously and easily along, being guided around obstacles and free to enjoy each moment in the comfort of that grace. Faith is the willingness to enter the stream, let go and become one with it so that we too can effortlessly move past obstacles on our own journey!

Chapter 10: October
October 2

Superhero

There is something indestructible in all of us! Somehow we human beings have a way to digest, interpret, recover from setbacks and pain and come out stronger by finding a blessing in the struggle. Pain, as unwanted as it is, is a call for the Superhero inside.

When the SOS goes out, the hero responds. So when we fail or are hurt, our Superhero jumps to the phone booth, takes off our glasses and emerges as Superman.

We need to open ourselves to the wonder of it all and we will emerge stronger. Seek and ye shall find' is the way of truth!

Chapter 10: October
October 3

Afraid of sadness

Mark Nepo frames one of the most valued statements I have wrestled with as follows 'are we so afraid of emotion, that any depth of feeling is called sadness?'

This is so true in observing our norms. Why do we not let ourselves dig deeper, feel the pain we suffer, recognize all is not right?

Society teaches us to be bigger, be stronger, to shake it off!

I was recently playing with my grandson at the playground. He has a want to be sensitive, so when he tripped on the Wooden play space and began to cry, I quickly told him to shake it off, walk through it, be a big boy? He continued to play limping a bit until the sight of blood scared us both. He was right, there was reason for pain, and I quickly got him home for some care.

I tell this story to magnify the biases of our societal norms. Too often we believe any reaction of pain or sadness is perceived weak or vulnerable.

This makes no sense. When we are sad, we can be sad. It has its purpose in how we develop. Recognizing 'what is', is the fastest way to our soul, denying it is the fastest way from our soul!

So, feeling the pain, being sad is a natural process that we must go through to heal most effectively and in fact make us stronger. It is better to go through the sadness than to deny its existence.

Chapter 10: October
October 4

The totality of the universe

No person exists alone. 'We all have the totality of the universe at our base and enlightenment makes that a conscious experience.' Lama Govinda

There are times, even when we are not trying that we connect to the largeness of the whole universe and we feel part of its glory. In those insights of time, which Lama Govinda calls 'enlightenment', we feel embraced by the oneness. We are warm, and peaceful.

These enlightened moments occur more when we are doing something outside ourselves like caring for a sick child and seeing the glimpse of hope, walking within nature and being overcome by its greatness, laughing out loud!

These moments are pointers to truth and where our essential spirits are all the time. Right there in front of us - at our base!

Chapter 10: October
October 5

Pain and wonder

We are hosting an African family fresh from the pain of abandonment in Sudan, and a long painful journey across the bush and then the world to return back home. I see the intersection of pain and wonder in their eyes.

Life is filled with these intersections and faith helps us see choices rather than dead ends or one ways. It is so easy to see only the pain.

In reality, there is always an intersection of wonder in deep pain! Wonder creates the space for the seeds of good to germinate. How did I get here? Where am I going? Where will this lead me?

When we can see an intersection of questions and wonder instead of a dead end, we see faith. Faith will help us get through it all and embrace the wonder that dwells among all things!

Chapter 10: October
October 6

Wind

We can experience wind in two ways. We can create it or feel it. If we are still, we will feel it come to us, even ever so slightly. We can also create wind by running or twirling or fanning ourselves!

The Holy Spirit, like the wind is alive in two ways. We can be still, and feel its ever presence or we can invoke the spirit by having intention in our thoughts and actions, like fanning ourselves or dancing and twirling!

In the intentional doing and being the spirit is present!

Chapter 10: October
October 7

Silence

I remember well a 2000 documentary about the lost boys of Sudan. When they somehow finished their long journey to refuge, a photographer so eloquently spoke about the deep silence among them. It was a deafening roar of nothing.

The African family that we are now offering a home has a two year old that is totally silent! There is something so rare and discomforting about a child being so still! Before she left on her journey, she was a talkative, curious 2 year old, and for some reason that we only can project, she just reflects and chooses silence.

Her movements are silent too, she creates no sound!

I believe in that silence she is being still and welcoming her spirit to return. She is experiencing everything that her soul is feeling. Silence is threatening to us who wish to protect children, but I am expecting it is God's way of finding her truth, living her pain and setting the background to be safe again.

Silence is a pathway to our souls. We are told through scripture to 'Be still and know that I am!' I am quite sure that our 2 year old friend has discovered this deep truth!

Days unknown

Ever wake up and go through your day in your mind? That seems to be a common practice of the mind and widely accepted as a best practice for a good organized life.

But in scripting the day too much, we may strip our day of the space necessary to be in spirit. Our days are filled with our plans.

Where would our days go if they had some free space? What connections, meetings, and helpful God incidences would we walk by or into? What unfolding before us would we miss entirely?

Consider the young traveler who plans no days. They just go! They buy an unlimited rail pass and make no reservations. Their journey is guided by the day as it unfolds, their itinerary is unknown and they don't have plans. If there is more to see, they stay where they are. If they engage a friend, they stay and explore with them! They leave total space for God to plan. That travel experience is full of life, adventure, surprises and connections.

Our Days are potentially just like that, waiting to unfold before us, unknown and yet full of potential. In real time, we need to strike a balance and keep enough time open in our days to allow God to work through us and reveal just what our purpose for that day is. Little by little the schedules will blend.

Chapter 10: October
October 9

Protecting what we love

A Zen saying goes like this. 'the pet swan is grown in a jar. As it grows, the swan cannot survive. The only way to free the swan is to break the jar and kill it'
This Zen parable speaks to protecting something we love so much, in the end, we kill it ourselves!

What do you protect? Is your protection leaving room for growth or is your protection stifling or limiting?

I use this parable to take a look inside to see what I am over protecting about me? What am I putting in a bottle? Do I protect my self so much, I do not let my heart grow? Am I restraining the expression of my love in favor of fitting in? Do I show myself differently than what I am?

Our human journeys are fragile. Our ego grows and protects what the ego believes is important and puts a bottle around our true self. Similar to the swan's bottle we will kill ourselves with that protection. We must let the ego go!

Chapter 10: October
October 10

What is it we do?

We are aware of so little. Radio or cell phone waves are flowing by us constantly, yet part of our consciousness only when we tune in!

Similarly, The waves from our enlightened universe are always there waiting for us to tune in! I liken the intention of 'doing' as a means of tuning into that frequency and create a moment where our hands and spirit connect. These moments become sacred, our doing brings joy and true happiness is ours.

Chapter 10: October
October 11

Being Downsized

In today's economy there is fear. I read that voluntary job shifts are at an all time low because people fear losing what they have and will not risk a change despite unhappiness.

Worry is everywhere and this cannot be good.

When life downsizes us, It is important to remember that our spirit remains constant, waiting to bring comfort and redemption to any worry or fear.
As we engage the spirit in these times, we work to true size ourselves through any fear, and our spirits voice and calling becomes clearer!

This true sizing is the right sizing of our souls and in the end will create redemption and growth.

Chapter 10: October
October 12

Being stiff versus supple

My wife is feeling the pains of disappointment, feeling left to bear the stresses of her choice to help this African family against all odds. This 'help' was not merely helping others, but was a major undertaking in support of a family in need from across a world of large barriers. It was a choice to stand tall and has brought both great joy and great pains!

There comes a time when the world challenges us to stand up for what is right. When this happens, Do we stand tall stiff or tall supple? The palm trees in confronting strong winds stand tall but supple. They will bend, they will lean and they will let the wind run through. The oak tree in contrast stands tall and stiff, almost in defiance, not giving in to the winds with its stiff trunk and leaves. The palms bend and don't break, the oaks either stand or fall!

In your storms, choose to stand tall like the palm. Bend and let the winds of pain through, do not attach or cling to them, merely watch them blow by and stand another day.

Chapter 10: October
October 13

Clinging

It is often our holding onto things so tightly that causes us more pain than the letting go.

I wish sometimes that we can sit and watch a movie of our life that shows a backdrop of how easily life flowed around us and how Gods' grace enveloped us fully every day! It would be amazing to see that when we try and manipulate the outcomes and control the events that come through our lives we tend to create stress and pain that was unnecessary. The movie would show the power of Gods' grace.

I wish it were clearer to us now. We can sit with joy knowing we are all held as Gods treasured gift. We need not cling to attachments that come and go, that we can just be!

Chapter 10: October
October 14

The pace of meditation

I often feel inadequate about centering, particularly when taking time to slow down seems impossible. I recall Eckhart Tolle saying that it is the awareness and not the time that counts in a meditation.

So, when we can become aware that we are disconnected from our soul, that alone is progress and in itself a meditation. That split second of seeing has created sacred space!

It takes just that second to create awareness to take a deep breath and align with our heart. Miracles reveal themselves in those sacred spaces. Our goal is to lengthen our awareness little by little and spend more time in that space!

Chapter 10: October
October 15

Carry something to give to others

There is a Holocaust survivor story that talks about a woman who saved a piece of bread every day just in case someone else needed it. This image defines the human spirit of giving beyond oneself as the ultimate gift of the spirit.

In doing so, we ourselves are fed by the spirit and quite literally can survive the in survivable. Many of us (thank God) will never experience such despair as the holocaust, but the lesson is there for us to absorb in our everyday despair that weighs us down.

When we can give outside ourselves we can define ourselves more than anything else. In just asking the question of ourselves, 'what can I give?' our spirit is engaged, and we can overcome any obstacle.

It is in that moment, that miracles are seeded to become reality!

Chapter 10: October
October16

Natural lessons

The lessons within nature are like reading a book!
Many teach us to be patient. One wonder of nature is the preponderance of options for life.

Just think about why there are millions of eggs that make one fish, or millions of pollen molecules to make one flower or millions of sperm to make that one child! Since nature is consistent in its actions, God must provide millions of paths or options for us too!

The infinite moments before us each day bring us many opportunities like the eggs for that one connection with our soul! Some pass by undetected, some will be eaten by our own ego, and some just do not survive! Some we pay attention to! I believe the secret to fulfilling God's purpose is intention!

In the many moments that occur each day, we need to pause and reflect on them before letting them go. Like capturing the moment that opens our purpose, the metaphorical fish egg God draws us to is meant for us on our path!

He persists to give us unlimited opportunities to live the life He wills! We need to be intentional only, and the moment will reveal itself as God intended.

Chapter 10: October
October 17

Reflex

I always had great reflex! Playing baseball came easy to me because I could react with what I know now was improbable speed and accuracy. So that 90 mph fastball did not overwhelm me.

What I know now too is the protective side of reflex! When emotions are thrown at me or life's curveballs hit, I merely reflect them.

I never learned to be slow enough to absorb the hit, sit with the curveball awhile or sit back and refrain from reacting altogether!

Life needs to be absorbed to be lived more fully. Hurts need to be chewed on and properly digested. Life needs to include an innocence of just being there and absorbing what is happening as well as reacting. The real reasons for interaction reveals itself in stillness not in reflex!

Chapter 10: October
October 18

It's not right

Some in my family are undergoing extreme financial stress. We've been there -- still there in many ways! The pain and worry is horrific. Our minds become satiated with worst-case scenarios. We let depression into our psyche and it does not leave easily. What to do?

I have fought mightily to overcome. I try everything within my power. Of this battle, I know this; I can make a difference in finding ways to survive on the material side. I can fight and scrape and piece together efforts to get by. I also know I can't beat the depression, I can't fight the worry,

I also learned I can do nothing of importance without God. Only God can provide a lasting peace that passes understanding. In truth, all the pain and the worries are impermanent. God's love is permanent and right.

Chapter 10: October
October 19

Migration

I was playing soccer with my grandson when a flock of geese flew over. "Getting ready to migrate" I thought. Their perfect V formation intrigues me to this day, particularly the switching of leadership positions so easily and smoothly.

The inner intelligence of animals to just do what they are genetically programmed to do amazes me every time.

I am keenly aware of how that same intelligence lies also in us! Through evolution we have tinkered a bit with this innate skill. As our brain has grown we have forgotten some of our callings.

We see pieces of our innate calling occurring in our life; whether a déjà vu experience, a thought that comes from nowhere, a change in plans for no obvious reason etc.   All these are connections with our inner spirit and signals to do what we are called to do!

When we are aware, when we turn into these truths, we can follow their path to enlightenment, when ignored we miss a great opportunity to see our purpose and we live unaware! We need to listen to our calling more.

Chapter 10: October
October 20

Erosion

We lived in SanFrancisco a long while ago. One of the most treasured trips we would take is the drive down the coast or through the Sierra Nevada Mountains.

Both are breath taking and awe filling with natural beauty. I think back now to the dichotomy of each side, to my left majestic mountains of great strength and to my right the ocean or the valleys. I drove the road between.

Nature works the rocks or peaks and erodes them down to nothing, sometimes bare. We ride the road of life in the same way! Lifting us up and then being worn down. It is in that ongoing process of erosion, of being worn bare that we reveal a new beauty and we are alive again!

Chapter 10: October
October 21

I don't understand

Thich Nan Hanh writes "if you tell me you understand I feel pessimistic, if you tell me you don't understand, I am optimistic"

The mere admission of not understanding reveals your openness and vulnerability.

When doing homework with my grandson, if he does not understand, I open every door I can to bring some light. We connect, we collaborate, and we struggle together because teaching is a hard skill! If he says that 'he understands', we move on and inevitably miss something.

This concept applies to our spirit life as well. In every day struggles with the meaning of life, if we admit to not understanding the deeper truths we open ourselves mysteriously toward a better understanding.

Chapter 10: October
October 22

Winter

Winter is coming quickly as I witness the shorter days coming upon us. We have a beautiful property and I feel blessed to have shared it for a while while here on earth.

Behind our home there is a fairly steep hill, to the right great views down to a pond, to the left deep woods. I always sought the beauty of the hill and the pond for solace. The woods to the left seemed dark and scary. I remember our first winter here when the darkness of the forest revealed itself without the cover of its leaves. A new beauty was upon me, the forest floor complete with the signs of life, death and resurrection. The winter light swirling through tall tree stands playing games with shadows and presenting a new beauty every bit as beautiful as the hill!

I recognized then that winter is freeing too! In our darkest winters we still can hold hope for a glittering resurrection and a wonderful transformation! No matter where that darkness comes from, the light is remarkably still there waiting to reveal the beauty beyond the night.

Chapter 10: October
October 23

Can you swim?

I was talking with my grandson about swimming. I told him I did not swim because I was afraid of water and never learned. He could not understand as swimming seemed so easy to him?

The conversation brought me back to my Aunt Cetta's boat. I must have been 4 or 5 years old and my aunt pushed me off her boat. I had a life jacket on, but the unexpected fall and going under water, which seemed like forever shocked me in many ways. I remember coming up to the surface screaming in fear and obviously traumatized to this day. I remember it well unfortunately!

I see the experience now within the context of the inherent wisdom of surviving. People react to painful events often by doing what I did, putting the pain away in a box and forgetting about it until direct or indirect situations call us back.

But life prefers we deal with the pain and learn. I could have learned to swim, overcome fears and been a better person as a result! The lesson of overcoming is something I now can treasure. Yet, I decided to be someone afraid of the water and whatever other pains I carried from that experience.

This storyline repeats in every life situation that we decide to store away rather than deal with the pain. Can you imagine the amount of stuff in that storage box for most of us?

In being forced to think about it now, I can see the gaps in my development that resulted. Each time we store a pain away rather than work through it, we also defer learning and put another layer of stuff between our souls and our consciousness. So, the innocent question 'can you swim' was ever so deep and revealing.

What questions trigger you in the same way?

Chapter 10: October
October 24

Nothing is lacking

Lao Tsu suggests the whole world comes to you when you lack nothing. The ability to be happy with what you have creates space for true joy. My wife and I were struck by the unexpected joy present in the refugee camps in Africa. Here were people forced from their homeland, persecuted and oppressed, nothing left in their material accounts, pride stripped, and you could argue their spiritual accounts were taken too! Yet, there was great joy! Why was this we asked ourselves, as it was so unusual, unexpected and un-American!

The secret we came to believe was in the stripping of attachments, nothing was being held onto, and nothing was of value except being with God and depending on God to survive? The refugees depended on the largesse of others through the UN and the sharing of anything to survive. They prayed often and in a way continuously. I likened it to first generation Christians and their eternal hope and great joy in knowing Jesus personally! The way things are was the way things are. They had nothing, yet had everything.

Chapter 10: October
October 25

False promises

How many promises have we made to ourselves that we break? Why is that?

If there is anyone we should be able to commit to, it should be ourselves. The gaps between what we say and do are sometimes so great we need to begin again, perhaps on another path.

In deeper truth we fall short time and again. Each promise needs to come from an inner truth or it will inevitably fail or fall short.

Chapter 10: October
October 26

Listen!

One of the more interesting things about the development of young people is to learn to listen. Our grandson brims with enthusiasm and he just can't wait to get out what is running around in his mind. Trying to teach the art of listening to others is like walking against a strong wind, there is a lot of effort, a lot of spinning and very slow progress!

God wants us to listen by putting His deepest lessons in quietness.   He also gave us two ears and one mouth, which should be a signal in itself to listen more. This is not easy learning!

Listening to the quiet is a paradox in itself! Yet, when we can quiet our minds, listening deepens our gifts, opens our hearts and reveals the spirit within.

Chapter 10: October
October 27

Space dive

Last week a man sponsored by a drink company jumped from a balloon capsule 123.000 feet above the earth, just at the edge of space. It was fascinating! He set some records and proved that an individual can break the sound barrier. I was taken by the view he had jumping from a position of seeing the globe and curvature of the earth!

Then at upwards of 900 mph he rushed toward earth in certain death if his parachute or anything failed. The beauty, majesty and stillness of the earth was replaced by frenetic speed, out of control spinning and outright worry for us watching him, let alone himself.

Then the parachute opened and more slowly and gently brought him to a safe landing. So is life! We prepare for what is coming to the best of our ability. We jump with a sense of faith. We go through the twists and turns, we are out of control for a while and somehow, in faith, we find some peace.

The God that is good is our parachute, carrying us softly to a better ending than we would have ever imagined.

Chapter 10: October
October 28

Try try again

Folklore teaches. This short parable of 'try, try again' reminds us we should never give up! In matters of the spirit, I see this more clearly as true just as it is said, like learning to ride a bike...we try and fail, we try again and again.

We get it at some point and the parable lives as we have interpreted it!

Chapter 10: October
October 29

The art of dancing

I know many people who had difficult childhoods and carry those pains as weights. Dancing with joy is just not possible for them.

I read a story about a young boy in South Africa who was caught dancing in the streets with crutches. The images are striking and tell us that we can shed the weights and dance regardless of what weighs us down.

The joy we bring to that moment, lightens the load even if for only that moment. God blesses the moments.

When we can string them together like the notes in a songbook, the pleasant note becomes a chord, then a set, and then a hymn, then we dance!

Chapter 10: October
October 30

Hollow-ween

I was driving yesterday and passed hundreds teenagers walking dressed in dark scary clothes with their faces painted gruesomely. It was very disturbing to me and I could not fathom the 'why'.

I believe Halloween has become hollow.

There seems to be no redeeming value in what our society has created and what kids act out. All Saints day and All Souls' Day were holidays of the church to bless those who came before us and set a positive role model with their lives. All Hallows' eve was in a way to bless their spirits.

When did we shift to gruesome and scary? The original creation of 'space' in our lives to honor those who have come before us is of value. To set up role models of a saint in God's eyes is what guides growth from generation to generation. I know we would be better off if we preserve the goodness versus the gruesome, the joy versus the despair, light versus fright!

Halloween has become hollow to me.

Chapter 10: October
October 31

Buddha meets Angulimala

There is this story where Buddha meets this prisoner who had killed others. After a long and mutual stare, the Buddha says 'I stopped, you did not!' Just what did

Buddha stop?

This question is powerful because it underlies all living. We are all the same was the Buddha's premise! This story got me thinking, When do we kill others? Does this happen in each of us? Can we project that 'killing' in every thing we do, is there the ability to stop or not?

Every human interaction has at its root a spiritual opportunity! In each one, we also have the ability to 'kill' or 'stop' in some way. Physically, we can affront by not paying attention, by abusing or oppressing even in the small things; we must stop. Mentally we can affront by looking down upon, by diminishing, by not listening; we must stop. Emotionally, we can affront by verbally discounting or abusing, by withholding; we must stop. Professionally, we can affront by selfish greed or the exertion of power that we perceive we have; we must stop. All these are little killings of the spirit that Buddha identifies. We must choose again and again, moment-by-moment to stop!

Chapter 11: November
November 1

Do it entirely, not well

Thomas Merton reflects that we do too much and when doing too much, we actually submit to violence upon ourselves. Mark Nepo further reflects to do one thing but do it entirely!

The word 'entirely' caught my attention. Among the many tasks on our agenda most days, pick one and do it entirely, staying away from the traditional thought of doing it well.

I like this because it brings us into the spirit of entirety and away from the ego of judging. This is a brilliant nuance. I will bring myself entirely to this moment, God takes it from there.

Chapter 11: November
November 2

Danger and opportunity

The Chinese ideogram for danger also means opportunity. How clever our ancient wisdom is! When danger finds us, we need to seek opportunity within the danger.

Somewhere in the course of events that confront us is the opportunity to break through and not break, somewhere there will be room for redemption.

Chapter 11: November
November 3

All Souls' Day

We went to a play tonight "Freud's last session" where he chatted with CS Lewis on the existence of God. Lewis made a key first point about the existence of our soul. "If you yearn for something naturally like milk as a baby or to swim if you are a duck, the milk and the water are real!"

"So, if you yearn to be joyous or happy, things of the spirit, God must be real."

Our souls call us.   Whether a yearning or even a Freudian slip, our soul finds ways to get our attention. Pay attention and God will be more real to you.

Chapter 11: November
November 4

Just one thought!

As we engage life fully, we constantly interact with others.   Just think of a standard day, and walk through the infinite opportunities to engage another human being and the question really is do we engage and make those moments sacred or just passing moments.

For example, let us walk through a shopping trip for groceries, which most people do often. First, there is the car ride; the stopping at stop signs, the many decisions of a right of way, the parking, the lady walking in front of you, the shopping cart selection, the store traffic, the passing of fellow shoppers, workers, products, the waiting in line, the cashier, the loading and unloading, the others leaving, and so on.

So, how many potential interactions did we have in that one mundane act of shopping and did we decide to engage with intention?

Each of those hundreds of opportunities were chances to create a sacred moment, and we most often miss them all!

What one thought can we bring to our ordinary day so that we can make it extraordinary and sacred. In doing so, we can create a richer life and forge a new path.

Chapter 11: November
November 5

Plans are useless

Winston Churchill said that plans are useless and planning is invaluable!

We believe we must have plans, but most often our planning no matter how good, does not turn out as we thought! If we could keep tabs on how our plans work, we would find that our plans always change just as everything around us changes!

So, planning is the more critical skill to have. Our planning needs to be flexible enough to engage life and prepare us to move where it calls us, rather than where we pre-disposed to be!

Plans need to prepare for the 'what ifs'! We need to understand that all choices open us to more choices!

When we are more open to engage the moments that come our way, our days will be more blessed.

Chapter 11: November
November 6

Squinting to focus

As my eyesight changes with age, I often squint to see more clearly. Squinting brings the focus onto the intended view. At the same time, squinting also results in greater focus on the specific item you target and other items seem to fade in the background.

The Sufi have an expression of seeing things through the 'hearts eye'. The hearts eye requires a broadening of the view, seeing more of the spaces around us to see the miracles. This is a better way to see, yet so rare. When we focus, we lose the surrounding story, we block the view of the spaces and in a spiritual way, we lose sight and remove any "wonder" from our view!

Open yourself to the miracles before us by seeing what surrounds what we normally see.

November 7

Waters within

Mark Nepo writes that as we age, we are more frequently worn by experience, and become like an inlet where waters wash more easily into us and they swell to tears more often!

As humans, we have come to fear tears and yet we should see the wisdom of the waters that flow into us and welcome tears as a pointer to the truth.

November 8

Gilgamesh and the stones

Gilgamesh, the Sumerian Hard King sought the immortal ones advice about the secret of life. The immortal ones response was to 'follow the stones' to the secret!

There were so many stones that Gilgamesh became frustrated with the obstacles on the journey, and he smashed the larger stones before him to make it easier to find the secret.   In doing so, he ruined his ability to follow the stones.

Often in our human experience we are hardened by obstacles rather than learning from them. We break away from relationships we need because they are perceived hindrances, we isolate when we need hugs.

In these things, we lose our markers to find the secret of life! Gilgamesh teaches us to be more flexible, more open, more patient while on our own path. The roadblocks we perceive may just be our pointers!

November 9

On the ride

We received some photos from our friends' son who is in Africa for a semester. The photos brought back memories of our own safari. The natural, unfiltered beauty of Gods world and the peace of existing precisely how God intended.

The oneness and holyness of every moment, even in the kill impressed me when we visited Africa. The universe moves so beautifully, peacefully, predictably in the natural cycles that are imbedded in all things.

We are in this incredible ride together and the more we can just be in the natural flow of the cycle, like the animals, the grasses, the trees, the waters...the better the ride!

Chapter 11: November
November 10

Seeking

St Francis prayer is famous for words of humility. "Seek not to be consoled, but to console" He also wrote less famously, that 'you are that which you are seeking!'

When we seek outside our soul for things we believe will heal us, like material possessions, attachments, we are missing the one true healing place of our inner soul!

The kingdom of God sits within us. When we seek that first, all things come to us and we become that which we seek!

Chapter 11: November
November 11

We are one

Kahil Gibran wrote (paraphrasing) that 'in every atom is found the elements of the universe, in each drop of water the secrets of all oceans, in each of us we find all aspects of life'!

This is the sustaining wonder of God and creation. In all things exist all things!

We keep learning as humans and we get deeper and deeper into the physics of this universe that there is an undercurrent of a grand intelligence and universal oneness. All things fit some design that is predictable, and all things are yet unknowable!

We are growing in knowledge enough to see that we (as human beings) are a part of the miracle. We are actually one with the trees and the air, one with the birds and the lions, one with our neighbors, one with God!

Today is my wife's birthday. In all the special gifts we experience through a soul mate, there is clarity in what we mean as oneness. All the world works as we work. I am grateful for the blessing of that oneness!

November 12

Taaora

One of the ancient Polynesian Gods Taaora created the world by successively growing within a shell and then needing to break that shell to create a part of the universe. I liken the story to our own creations. How many shells are we forced to break to create a new 'us'.

Knowing the twists and turns of living have always been accompanied by times of despair and growth, we can retroactively see the shells being grown to protect us and than shattering to allow us to grow! We all live many shells in our life! Each self that is created with each breaking shell becomes more enlightened by the growth of the last! The final self dwells with God.

Those broken shells are signs of creation along the way!

November 13

Almost rope

I heard this comedian, Steven Wright talking about the marketing of string! 'If you need string buy this string! It's so good it's almost rope!' I laughed out loud at the punch line!

I got to thinking that the strong rope that holds mega tankers to docks is thousands of intertwined pieces of string!

To become rope, we must marry our string together in a pattern that creates one strong bond! Our spirit with our thoughts, our mind and body, our doubts and dreams, our heart and hands! We are born string, but I prefer to think of us all as 'almost rope!'

We are a work in progress. We are all string, yet almost rope! When we understand this oneness, we have the supreme strength of knowing we are rope together!

November 14

Be here now

I was talking to a colleague in a large company who said his company has started training every employee to give them permission to 'be here now'!

This is unbelievable! Basically the company was saying focus on the moment, don't multi task, be where you need to be fully! This is potentially a seminal moment in our world. 'Be here now' is the one truth underlying living in the present moment!

We cannot split ourselves and expect to be whole. We cannot look into anothers soul if we are distracted, we cannot walk in nature with thoughts elsewhere, we cannot just be here if we are really there!

Chapter 11: November
November 15

Tootsie rolls

Knowledge and familiarity help take fears away. Those that have survived a cancer scare or had a near death experience tell us they now live more fully.

I can see the sense of that, believing that if you know death and do not fear death, life can take on more value. More often than not, that experience finds its way to focusing on the now as the 'way' for those that tell the story.

Every fear is like a tootsie roll pop, when we work with it and get to know it, stay with it for awhile, we find a surprise peace at its center, and we more fully can enjoy that peace!

Chapter 11: November
November 16

The Talmudic tale

A Rabbi is talking to his students about understanding when the first moment of dawn arises. After a few missed metaphoric opportunities and wrong answers, the Rabbi circles his students in silence.

'The dawn arises when you first see yourself in another persons eyes'.

The oneness of the universe connects us all in many ways, and in a way connects us to all things, not just one another! Consider the discovery of DNA and how science has found remarkable sameness between us and any other thing, not only each other! We can gain great comfort understanding this paradox to be our window to a greater belonging. We are not just a drop of water, we are the ocean!

As a result of that perspective, We are never journeying alone even when we feel so, fore everyone is on the same journey, feeling the same pains and fears, moving along with the tides together, sometimes feeling like that single drop of water rather than part of the huge ocean.

When we feel that oneness our dawn arises!

Chapter 11: November
November 17

Worn leaves

As the leaves fall, I sometimes try and catch them! When I was younger, that was one of my most memorable games to play! I didn't catch many, but when I did, I would take a look at each leaf and see the many variations and markings there were that made them unique like a fingerprint.

Our heart has similar markings of our life like the leaf; colors of joy, signs of wear and tear and sometimes the marks of disease.

We are both living beings. It would be lightening if we could shed and renew every year like the leaf.   What is wearing you down right now? What disease is lurking that you could reverse?

Let the renewal of fall happen, feel lightened by the shedding of your leaves, than renewed as you anticipate the great signs of spring!

Chapter 11: November
November 18

Bronte

My dog was the best companion. I saw a commercial today with a dog doing the same thing with their owner from a puppy to old age.

I fondly remembered Bronte in that precise way! From a puppy to 17 years old she connected with me every day. No moment escaped her intentional 'being', no moment did I not feel her. I learned a lot from her.

In her last months I gave up sleeping well, carried her up and down stairs, guided her in both hearing and sight loss. There was never a question that I would be there for her. Expressions of love were just moments to her. She was a living example of pure consciousness! I am forever joyful for her and I cherish those sacred visits she now blesses me with!

Chapter 11: November
November 19

Ariadne and Theseus

I am reading Greek mythology to my grandson. I believe the gruesome exterior of the stories remind him of superhero stories, so he is engrossed! Theseus is sent into the labyrinth to be killed by the Minotaur.

Knowing the danger of getting lost in the labyrinth as every bit as lethal as the great Minotaur, he skillfully breaks down a valued gift of a fabric Ariadne weaved for him. He lays the thread down on his way in and uses the thread made by Ariadne to find his way out of the labyrinth when he was ready!

Sometimes we need to break down parts of our own perceived treasures and leave a trail as we face our own Minotaur inside the labyrinth?

Then, free of the labyrinth and free of the attachment to something impermanent we are free to love.

Chapter 11: November
November 20

Risk and faith

I am in the midst of another risky venture. I sometimes sit and think about why I do this?

Then a wave of power and worry comes over me and I realize that in anything risk requires faith. When you venture forward without knowing a result that is bringing faith on, head on!

Taking risks is the essence of being committed. I remember the gift of seeing birds taught to fly by their parents. Without jumping in faith they would never lift. Without leaping forward in faith, we would not experience our own growth, whether that is in love, skills, or spiritual depth. Risk is everything!

Chapter 11: November

November 21

Almost or already?

Most among us reach a point on their journey that they can go no further. We don't talk much about these shortened incomplete journeys.

Both the marathon runner who hits the proverbial 18 mile fictional wall, or the mountain climber who falls to their knees in exhaustion at 12,000 feet starving of oxygen finished a remarkable feat of almost.

In the almost, there is the likelihood of knowing the truth as much if not more than those who finish the challenge. At the end of the day, everything there is, is wherever we are!

All people on their journey reach these points of choice, many go on to fulfill their goal, and many leave short, some die in the trying. I believe we need to go no further than where we are, stop, take in the spectacle of our miracle and be one with God.

This matters not whether our journey brings us to our garden, in a marathon race, on a mountaintop or in a hospital. First stop, embrace the miracles all around, smile and be with God for a while. That journey is the triumph of the soul and it is available to all of us already!

Chapter 11: November
November 22

Only spirit can recognize spirit

When we lived in San Francisco I loved to take walks amongst the tall redwoods in Muir woods. It was like being in a wonderful church, where God unmistakably stood in physical form.

It was then I now know my spirit recognized spirit!

There is a specific leap of the heart that is shared when the two meet and my spirit did so with the trees! There is a peace that overwhelms you and there is a knowing that is shared in each spirit-to-spirit moment.

This spirit-to-spirit recognition awaits us not just in the wonder of life's majesty but in every interaction of life. We need take the intentional time of walking into the moment like walking into the redwood forest! Your heart will leap and your joy will expand.

Chapter 11: November
November 23

Giving thanks

We attended grandparent's day for our grandson's school today. The teacher read the 'giving tree', a story of such unconditional love that the tree literally gave its heart and soul to the boy. Even in the end, despite little gratitude from the boy, the tree was happy!

There is something about a grandchild that relives the giving tree story. We too are happiest when giving of ourselves completely without expectations of return.

Chapter 11: November
November 24

Sacred order

I sat in my car marveling at the leaves fall from the tree in rapid succession. My first thought was that the sacred order was given, it is time!

The longer I live, the louder these orders become to me. I find myself connecting as if I am also given the order to take heed, the glory of God is passing through.

In these times, I find myself a participant in the order and not just the observer. I find truth in all things sacred, and I find all things sacred!

Chapter 11: November
November 25

Compassionate to yourself

Lao Tsu says to be compassionate to yourself you reconcile all beings in the world to you.

The sacred order includes the layers of invisible activities occurring all around us.

When we know the connection of all things as truth, we can begin to comprehend the power of the universe.

The great redwoods who stand so majestically above the earth, beneath they are all connected through their roots. When one feels stress, they all feel that stress and in a way communicate and console each other.

We human spirits are all connected the same way. When we are compassionate to ourselves, we are to all and in that recognition we reconcile all people to ourselves.

Chapter 11: November
November 26

Enter the kingdom

Jesus identified so many obstacles to entering the kingdom, I first read those as beyond possible, like a camel going through the eye of a needle!

A lesser known parable sheds some light on this is 'making the two one.'

Jesus knew that because of the development of our ego's, we were in some form two people! The two must become one! How do we do that?

We need to recognize that ego, that person we identify ourselves as, is not us! Our indweller, our Holy Spirit inside is the true us! The "us" that comes forth when we can put our ego aside and make room!

Jesus likens that objective to impossible actions because we must give up the attachments and false self we have known and hang onto. This is so hard, yet until we do, we cannot enter the kingdom.

Chapter 11: November
November 27

Morning has broken

Morning has broken like the first morning! Each day we toil through the hours fighting the grit that lives in life, and at times being overwhelmed by the challenges against our spirit, it tends to weigh us down.

Then, no matter how exhausted, at the end of the day, we sleep. This is Gods way of giving us pause and enabling our spirits to meditate through the lessons of the day.

Then morning breaks like the first morning, a miracle unfolds, light returns again and again! We come through like a daily baptism rested, the grit cleansed, and we are ready for another day!

Sacred windows

We visited a museum exhibit of the sacred windows. A small church found six Tiffany windows in an attic that had been removed from their church a hundred years or so ago. They lovingly had them restored and displayed!

In the process of taking apart, and cleaning the masterpieces, they took videos for all to see the painstaking process. I learned that stained glass has three layers of glass. I also learned that the cutting, coloring, drawing, layering is a complex artistic process.

To get to the point of being able to turn a complex dark window into an explosive show of light is remarkable.

We each are like stained glass! We are shaped by so many small and sometimes broken pieces. We have layers creating who we are, and yet when put in the light, we shine from the inside and we are beautiful.

Angels among us

I am convinced angels are here in our physical world. How many times have you felt something you could not explain, or recognized an interaction as special?

Here is one example. We don't see hummingbirds much, even with feeders they come and go with such speed; you enjoy the twittering visits for a moment and wish for more. This past summer, my wife was working on a serious life or death project to return a family stranded in Sudan. It was a miracle filled series of events.

On the first day of the trauma, a hummingbird came in front of our kitchen window and sat on a twig near our feeder. My wife took it as a sign of healing and that Chol, a recently lost soul she bonded with was guiding the events in some way. Well, the next day the hummingbird returned and for hours on end we would have the miracle of the hummingbird in direct sight! This went on for roughly six weeks.

On the day the family in Africa was put on a plane back to the states, the hummingbird was gone. She or he has not returned since. Whatever the explanation of how this attraction happened it is a convincing argument that something outside our understanding of the physical world occurred.

Angels exist.

Chapter 11: November
November 30

Precious things

There is a power in the things we hold precious. In the letting go, that power is released to the universe to use! My wife teaches me in ways she has no clue.

In the recent project to help the family stranded in Sudan, I found this story out after the fact. Before the family left, my wife's intuition saw danger. She gave our friend her gold cross necklace to be with her on her journey. After much turmoil, intrigue and terror the family returned safely and as it turns out just in time for the health of the children.

On one of the arranged phone calls during the escape process, my wife learned of the power of the cross and how our friend found strength in holding it and feeling empowered to persevere.

You must know that tiny cross was very special to my wife, yet in the giving of something so precious a power to heal was released across the universe and made available to the family far, far away. I did not find out until months later that the cross was never returned. It mattered not to my wife, the intended power of protection and healing had occurred! In the giving away of what we hold dear, we release the power of the spirit!

Chapter 12: December
December 1

Do dreams matter?

I look at our grandson and love the person he is becoming. He, like most kids have dreams of whom they want to be when they grow up.

Dreams are magical pieces of who we are, and the seedlings of what we can become. Our grandson wants to be a superhero. At this point, I am pretty sure that won't happen in his definition but it is influencing who he will become. He looks up to those who help others, he has compassion, he is selfless in a lot of ways, he is kind, and he is funny. His next dream will again have some key parts that will help him become his true self.

As adults we dream with attachments and instead of moving on to our next dream when the first one does not happen, we feel pain in the loss.

We need to see our broken dreams just as if we were the children again. They are likely our spirit self-helping us become our true self. All steps toward our purpose are dreams and they matter in every instance.

Dreams are the seedlings of that reality, and pointers we must follow. In pursuing them we will find true peace and experience the joy of becoming.

Chapter 12: December
December 2

Reveal or live the revelation

This simple statement and what it means to live revelation strike me in a deep way. I started writing this series of reflections because I was inspired by Mark Nepo's poetry and how he revealed truth in such a powerful way based on how was living revelation!

Life is quick to differentiate between revealing a truth and living the revelation. It is a higher order that we enter life and live its promise.

Chapter 12: December
December 3

Mother Theresa

In our lifetime we all were blessed to witness a Saint in Mother Theresa. This woman exhaustively provided Gods hospitality to the least fortunate among us and she gave those she helped hope and dignity.

How do we ever get close to those ideals?

Yet, in reality, we are already there. Mother Theresa said she saw God in every one of her charges.

We are all saints inside! That gift of compassion that Mother Theresa showed the world exists inside of us all, we too can see the face of God in everyone!

Everyday we have hundreds of opportunities to live into that sainthood. Every moment gives us the chance to be more hospitable, caring and compassionate, we only need to choose to be present.

We too are saints waiting to be released!

Chapter 12: December
December 4

What should I be?

I remember well going to college and majoring in engineering because I was good in math and science and the jobs were projected to be there upon graduation.

I have no regrets because I fortunately morphed my way into doing what I love every day. Yet, thinking back, I would have benefitted more without pre-judging destiny and fate.

I believe work and passion and work and life are labels we have created that make no sense. The world needs people to be, not necessarily to be something.

We need to bring joy and passion and be alive and the world will be a better, healthier place fore our presence.

Chapter 12: December
December 5

Fencing and parrying a strike

My grandson is taking fencing lessons. I watched the last few weeks and I witnessed some interesting strategies. First, when an opponent lunges for a strike, the defense strategy is to parry or set aside the strike by using its own momentum to glance it off course.   In doing so, concurrently lunge yourself for a strike.

I thought how clever to use the energy of an obstacle to create an opportunity.

The following week, he learned the counter to the defensive parry. When you see the parry coming, in an ever so slight circular motion you can reverse the momentum of the parry in your favor and complete your own strike, using the energy of the parry to your advantage.

In every life situation we can turn the obstacle that confronts us (the negative energy) into a friend by using its own energy for good. Try parrying someone's negative energy with positive energy, the reflection will be positive.

Chapter 12: December
December 6

Burning colors into pottery

Ancient potters had some magic. Somehow, they painted colors into porcelain with an innate talent of patience and knowing. The colors that lay upon the wet clay need to dry layer by layer and they seep into the clay muted and blended. Only upon firing does the color emerge and the miracle unfolds for all to see.

The molding of our life's clay is similar. The layers are the grit of life, the daily grind. Each day we add color in some way. The color only emerges when we engage our soul like a kiln and add intention to those layers of color.

It is then that our layers of grit can be blended, softened, cleaned and emerge as a beautifully painted bowl or a colorful tapestry that we call a life well lived!

Chapter 12: December
December 7

Cloud cover

I watched the sun's rays come through a thinness in the clouds with a joy of anticipation in my heart. I thought how the walls we build around us are like cloud cover and they block our light from shining and to what good end?

Jesus said a lamp covered is not going to light the world. I can see my own cloud cover in certain circumstances, those walls around me that prevent my light from shining.

I believe that being aware is a spiritual way of creating a thinning of the walls. I still have not and perhaps never will be able to break through the walls completely, but I have a joyful anticipation that they are thinning enough where some light is streaming through for others to see.

Chapter 12: December
December 8

Labels

The course in miracles says we need to first unlearn everything we learned to feel the oneness of life.

One of the exercises in that course is to see all things as they are, not as we label them. It is eye opening. The chair is only a chair because we labeled it that.

In reality it is a living organism, with the same atomic structure, with aliveness inside regardless how rigid it appears on the outside. Eventually we realize we are one with the chair, one with the trees, one with the universe. We are the drop of water in the ocean, we are the grain of sand on the beach, we are the sub atomic energy of the earth within the vastness of the energy of the universe, we are love within love.

And so it is!

Chapter 12: December
December 9

Mark

I am reading Mark (bible gospel writer) from a historical perspective. I have come to explore some mysteries i was not in tune with before. Why did Mark write so late? Why did he write in Greek? Did he even write it?

The work of love is not a straight line and it needs to understand the perspective of that time. It is proposed by biblical historians that Mark wrote around 70AD. This is shortly after the Romans destroyed the temple and Judaism was being squashed by their military might.

It must have been an Armageddon experience where a million plus were slaughtered and the literal home of God was destroyed.

The not yet named Christians had their own thoughts and worries. Post temple, Jesus' words of "tear down this temple and I will rebuild in 3 days" was now clearer and in fact the only thing to hold onto for some. For survival of the Jewish faith something had to be done, perhaps the Jews who followed Jesus' ways seemed safer in moving a half step away from Judaism.

Whatever was really going on, it appears that Jesus' words became even more alive and a new energy to document this was undertaken by asking the 'witnesses' to document the story. They perhaps felt a need to make sure the story was saved and told. It is here that both the Jews and Christians realized God lives outside the temple building and inside the temple of our bodies.

Chapter 12: December

December 10

Story lines and wisdom

Our culture today acts upon story lines, quick snippets of information, twitter like statements that cannot possibly tell the whole story, and in fact often are a way to spin truth and win people to the writer's point of view.

Ancient cultures depended on stories to pass life's wisdom and convey learning and truth. There was wisdom in ancient mores that used stories to convey what was important and lasting. They were often repeated verbatim generation upon generation. They required time to sit, listen and distill value with the guidance of the wise one telling the story. The MZEE in African tribes!

What a different perspective today. Story lines and snippets rule the information flow. Imparting wisdom from a trusted elder has been replaced by snippets from an unknown writer.

Worse, when we seek to tell the longer story, we lose listeners to the culture of quick, lively, entertain me types of sharing information!

There is no time to share wisdom and truth. We must change that.

Chapter 12: December
December 11

Finding happiness

Great spiritual leaders say that happiness is fleeting or not easy to find in ourselves, but all agree it is impossible outside ourselves!

So why do we continue to look elsewhere for happiness? There is a treasure inside our souls. Our ego, (attachments, labels, pain bodies) blocks our access to our own treasure.

It is like we are standing in shallow flowing water with the treasure at our feet, yet the constant movement of the water, the swirling and churning of mud, the currents pushing us one way or the other prevent us from seeing our treasure.

Be still and seek the treasure inside. There is a peace in knowing it's there. In stillness even the unclear waters clear. We can let go of attachments that are not lasting, we can become aware of those pain bodies that drive discontent and give them space to lessen the grip on our soul. We can remove labels and judgment and begin to see our sameness with all things.

Then in clear still water our treasure awaits!

Chapter 12: December
December 12

Death defies all we know

When we die, our spirit lives in a new and unknown world. Consider this possibility of the after physical life.

Our spirits are weightless, and an energy that works in a way and a speed beyond human knowing. Time falls away completely as Einstein hypothesized when we reach that speed.

So in effect, we pass to the present moment. We experience only the love of God for all time. That is a wonderful picture. I will stop there!

Chapter 12: December
December 13

Jesus and the end of time

In this end of the calendar year, and beginning of the church year there are a couple of Jesus' sayings that I have reflected upon with more depth.

Paraphrasing the first from Revelation, as 'this generation will see these terrible signs and the end of time. The son of man will come on clouds to save his people' and the second as 'tear down this temple, and I will rebuild it in three days'.

The first is the classic Armageddon prophesies, and the second is often interpreted as prophesy of Jesus rising on the third day! In Jesus time, the Jewish people were once again heavily oppressed, but this time by a powerful global Roman Empire.

In 30 years from when Jesus said these words, the Jews would be in full-scale war with the Romans. In victory the Romans tear down the temple to end these Jews claims of their own kingdom, over one million Jews were killed, clearly an end of time tragedy of huge human and spiritual proportion.

The temple, where God resides was gone; the holiest of holies that was the backbone of the faith for thousands of years was destroyed! If Jesus was foreseeing this and He was clear of the disdain He had for the oppressions he witnessed, that surely would be the end of time to end all times!

Jesus also said he can rebuild the temple in three days during his last week In Jerusalem. People scoffed and elders decided that this Jesus character had to be dealt with. What if those two sayings were linked In a prophetic way?

If so, Jesus was prophesying the destruction of the temple. He was also identifying himself as the savior that is already present, but not recognized as such by the Jews.

Jesus would be the one to come on clouds to save His people by virtue of the empty tomb and rebuild the temple on the third day! We can imagine that upon the actual destruction of the temple these words made more sense, and the followers of Christ in some way were energized.

This explains to me why the gospels were written then and not before as it was seen as a survival of the faith to not only get the word out but sanctify them for all time.

The risen Christ would replace the temple and the temple (God) resides inside each of us, inside the temple of our souls. His rising and every day presence in the spirit was the coming in glory we foresaw!

I can hear Jesus' message distilled to its simplest form. "We need not follow all those rules and laws and physical attachments. God dwells inside you as the Holy Temple (Spirit), love your neighbor as yourself and follow me, I will give you rest!"

Chapter 12: December
December 14

Unsayable sayings

The word God is a label that cannot possibly be described by our human minds.

We cannot fathom the love and depth with words, so the truth or depth is really unsayable. The early Jews knew that and never said the word God. All the terms of sacred wisdom fall short of explanation.

We spend our whole life searching the mystical, building wisdom and learning what to say until paradoxically we cannot speak. We have learned that the revelation of the mystery is found in silence and in the spaces between words not the words themselves.

Chapter 12: December

December 15

Singing in the rain

Our grandson has taken to singing and dancing lately. We are not sure from where it comes but it certainly is a free expression.

I cringe every time I try to corral him in as I feel I am suppressing his song to fit my image of a well-behaved young man. Giving voice to joy is critical to surviving and living in joy.

If we limit our voice, we will have nothing to give and the world will be a dark silence.

Chapter 12: December
December 16

We have it all

There was this sage who approached this deeply troubled man, "my friend, there is great anguish in your soul, I wish to help you. He then said you may have a map or a boat".

The young man looked about him, saw the troubled people and things all around him and asked for the boat! The sage said, " Alright then, go! You are a boat, and life is the sea!"

Happiness can be found in whatever you choose.

Chapter 12: December
December 17

Where is joy without hope?

In many a present moment there is great despair. Hope is gone.

For those of us who have been there, it is a scary and sad time. But as those who have come through exhaustion know, where you are you will find all you need.

Rick Warren the great pastor of Saddleback church and author to a Purpose Driven Life has just added two chapters to his book. They reflect what he has learned about purpose himself from others!

Two things prevent purpose from being fulfilled; envy or wanting what someone else has or wanting to be someone or somewhere else!

Happiness only comes from who and where you are, so wanting something outside yourself is a recipe for hurt!

You need nothing else than what you have, you need to be only who you already are, happiness exists already in that sacred space. Be joyful in that knowing.

Chapter 12: December
December 18

Speaking in tongues

This movement has slowed a bit. I remember being in a service of evangelicals where someone started shouting noise. There was much praising The Lord in support for this person who was overcome by the spirit.

I sat questioning versus praising. Today I look back and smile at the fear present in me at that time. When we speak from anywhere it is a joyful expression of lifting our Holy Spirit to the world for all to see.

We give voice to our oneness to and with all things. Our speaking need not be words and need not be sound. It is important we give voice to our inner sacredness in some way that nourishes our soul. Speak and be glad in any tongue.

Chapter 12: December
December 19

Beethoven and Goya

These two giants of art have something in common. They lost their hearing and still created works of art after the fact.

Beethoven is said to have continued to create by listening to the vibrations, which was a real victory of the spirit.

Goya on the other hand painted his best after hearing loss! Why was that? It is conjectured he was now deaf to criticism and painted from his soul without fear of judgment.

Our individual light can be diminished or covered by criticism too. We need to make sure our light fills the dark and is not covered by circumstance or someone else. We are then free to be!

Chapter 12: December
December 20

The fork in the road - now what

When you come to the fork in the road, take it. Yogi Berra the great Yankee baseball catcher stated.

This gives me great solace. It speaks to moving forward without fear or judgment, and without regret for the choice not taken.

I am convinced that God is in every one of our daily interactions. He guides us to notice and be there with Him. We choose the proverbial 'fork' with every choice, yet with each choice we make, God lays before us more choices to keep us on the journey He wishes to guide us through.

 The good news is that He is there still!

Chapter 12: December
December 21

Only love dispels hate - Buddha

This is another universal truth. The individual hurt can be healed by forgiveness and love. Knowing can heal the pain of bias and judgment. In knowing another's soul you see the oneness and connectedness of each and bias loses power.

Love consumes hate, like light consumes dark. In the fullness of love, hate cannot exist.

Chapter 12: December
December 22

Find the source

An old Sufi tale goes like this. The caveman was thirsty. He noticed a small muddy stream flowing, so he followed it upstream. He got to the opening of a cave, took a light and followed the stream into the dark cave until he found its source and clear, clean water!

When troubled and finding ourselves in muddy waters, we should remember to not drink of the dirty water but trace the source. In the journey, we will have to navigate our darkness by shining a light on the muddy stream as we trace its origins until the source is found.

At that point, the mud settles, the darkness lightens, the waters are clear and life is giving.

Chapter 12: December
December 23

The big picture

Our first cruise was met with an unexpected storm. The squall tossed the boat as if we were in a bathtub with two kids playing boat wars. I tried to hold up in our stateroom, but being inside was not for me. I went out on deck and viewed the horizon. I immediately felt better looking at the bigger picture.

Somehow, the broader view gave a peace to the storm. I look back now and see the parallels to life. All our storms need perspective; all need a steady horizon that is always there, sort of our God giving us balance and a faith that this too shall pass.

Keeping the larger view is understanding that good is found in all things, life is not a storm, it is experience for a better tomorrow. The horizon is always there.

Chapter 12: December
December 24

Child's eyes see more

I love to listen to our grandson as he imagines himself with play into many things. I know the child sees things clearly, without filter - Godlike.

We need to begin to see things again like a child; talk to the birds, swing with the trees, smile with the suns rays, see the spirit inside almost anything!

It is that "insight" that brings us closer to God.

Chapter 12: December
December 25

Christmas morning has broken

Like the first morning, each day is a new miracle to behold.

Blackbirds have spoken like the first bird! Jesus came some 2000 years ago and broke a new morning with His 'way'! Follow His way, it's the best Christmas gift.

Chapter 12: December
December 26

We can't do that

One of the mysteries of life is the fact that the world will do quite well without us, yet we are pulled to change it!

There is no possibility we can solve the worlds problems because we look at them with the view of a changer rather than the changed. Ghandi said 'become the change you want to see in the world'!

We cannot fix starvation, but we can feed each other, we cannot stop violence but we can offer peace to our neighbor, we cannot stop loneliness but we can hold a friend. In this subtle nuance of being changed ourselves, we best can change the world.

Chapter 12: December
December 27

Squeezed of life

There is a silent worry in our lives that sets us back from living freely. When we are on the edge in any way, economically, emotionally, physically; we lose sight of the joy we once knew.

I liken it to being squeezed slowly by invisible stressors that keep us from being balanced. We imagine the stressors away trying to feel whole, yet at the first sign of slipping they come back tighter, removing air from our lungs and joy from our hearts.

It is only true faith that can take the worry away. In letting go and knowing something better is just around the corner, or right at our feet, or in eternity, we loosen the strain.

Then one day we look back and ask why we wasted so much time worrying. If only we knew!

Chapter 12: December
December 28

Moments outside ourselves

In the daily string of moments, we sometimes stay inside the one we are in! It is then that something happens that we can't explain. Like swaying to the music, we become the music. Walking in the field, we become the field. Gazing at the stars we become the universe.

For that brief moment we became one with our experience, we believed we were part of something larger, we were happy, we were staying in the moment, and when we do, we live through them, we feel joy.

When we live past them we feel lack.

Chapter 12: December
December 29

Que sadit

The African greeting in South Sudan has no direct interpretation. In thousands of years it has come to mean many things around a greeting. I like the 'hey, I care about you' interpretation. What a wonderful way to affirm each other's value.

To reflect on the soul in the greeting builds both people up to stay in the moment. I remember well when the lost boys of Sudan first came to the USA, they would sit for hours in the moment. Physical time meant nothing to them, only the engagement of another.

That time is long gone for them as they adjust to the rigors and stressors of western life.

What we could learn if we opened ourselves to say 'hey,I care about you!' And then spend the time like you meant it!

Chapter 12: December
December 30

Blind to the light?

God blesses those without a sense with extreme capabilities in other senses to compensate.

It is this miracle that opens to me the fact we know nothing of our capabilities and our senses. We have so much more to learn about our world, how it works and our role in it.

I am convinced that there must be a parallel world on another sense level that will someday exist for us all.

Chapter 12: December
December 31

I see

Marianne Williamson said that whenever we feel stress in a situation we are seeing something wrong. In the quest for inner peace, this is a powerful truth.

If we can change our view of the situation and find love, the stress will dissolve.

Consider this; if I pray for my enemy, one of two things will happen, they will either change or I won't care! Both relieve the stress I was feeling.

Seems like a simple truth we can work with.

Made in the USA
Middletown, DE
25 June 2015